Microsoft®, Access®, Word®, Excel®, Outlook®, and PowerPoint® are registered trademarks of Microsoft Corporation.

Conventions used:

Keyboard:
Keys to be pressed are enclosed in parenthesis such as: press (Enter).

Text to be typed, when included in an exercise step will be shaded. For example:
Type *No Fault Travel* and then press (Enter).

Mouse Operations:

Click: refers to clicking the left mouse button

Right-click: refers to clicking the right mouse button

Drag: refers to holding the left mouse button down and moving the mouse

Be sure to visit out our website: www.Pro-aut.com to order these workbooks in quantity.

Published by:

Pro-Aut Training and Consulting, Inc.
1024 Hemlock Ave.
Lewiston, ID 83501

You can also visit: www.LutherMaddy.com to contact the author, or see other resources available for this workbook.

Access 2013 The Basics

Table of Contents

Lesson #1: Basic Database Design

In this lesson you will learn:

Database Terminology
Basic Database Design
Relational Database Design

Lesson #1: Basic Database Design

Access Terminology

A database is an organized collection of information. Access makes it easy not only to organize data but also to manipulate and analyze the data it contains. You need to be familiar with a few database terms before you learn how to use a database.

Field: A field is a piece of information such as a First Name, City, or State. The field is the most basic element of an Access database.

Record: A record is a collection of related fields. An example might be a table of clients. Each record stores all information about a client in fields such as: First Name, Last Name, Street Address, City, State, Zip Code, Phone Number, and Birthday.

Table: A table is a collection of records with the same fields, as in our example of a client table. The records consist of rows in the table and the fields are the columns. For example, a table named Employees would be expected to only include company employees.

Database file: The database file is a collection of related tables. The file also contains the other Access database objects such as the Forms, Queries, Reports and Macros that comprise a specific database.

Primary Key: The primary key 🔑 is a field containing unique identifying information for each record, such as an identification number or social security number. Access uses this field to locate a specific record. Primary keys also allow you to relate tables. Although not commonly used, a primary key may also be the combination of more than one field.

Query: A query is an Access object that allows you to specify which fields and records you want to see. Queries are often used as the basis of reports. The query selects the records and fields to view and the report allows you to enhance the appearance of the resulting list produced.

Form: A form is a way to view, enter, edit, or print records in a table. You can design the form to match existing forms you already use.

Report: Reports allow you to present and view selected information in a meaningful way. The most common report layout organizes the information in columns. You can use reports to create totals and sub-totals.

Database Design

When you begin to create an Access database, think before you act. You should spend considerable time designing the database before you even start Access. The database design includes the tables and the fields they contain. You also need to establish the relationship between the tables.

Ideally, the design should be complete before you start using the database to prevent important tables or fields from being left out. Although Access allows you to change the design of a working database, you will often need to modify the forms, reports, and queries that refer to the table or tables which have been changed.

Changing the design of a database in use is often time consuming and difficult, depending on the number of existing forms, reports, and queries. Remember the old adage, *a stitch in time saves nine*. Plan for every possible use of the database during the design phase: every question it might be asked and every report that might be wanted before you begin to create the database.

Relational Database Design

Access has relational database capabilities, which means it can link or relate two or more tables. Relating tables allows Access to look up information from either table when needed.

A well designed relational database design saves in the duplication of information. With an invoicing database, instead of entering a customer's name and address each time he or she makes a purchase, you can store customer information in a separate *Customer* table. When you create a new invoice stored in the *Invoices* table, the *Invoices* table needs to contain a field that links to the specific customer record in the *Customers* table, often a customer number.

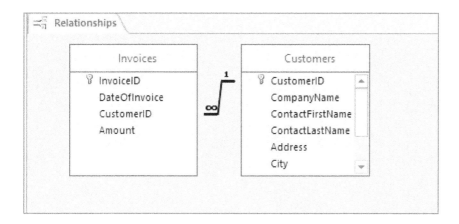

To relate two tables, each must have one field in common. This field must also be the primary key in the table representing the "one" of the "one to many" relationship. In this invoicing example, one customer may have many invoices.

Relating these two tables saves having to enter the complete customer name and address on each invoice each time he or she places an order. If you find yourself duplicating the same information, your database design is suboptimal.

Relational databases also allow you to maintain historical data. In the invoicing database, you have a record of every invoice your customers have. This process is referred to as normalization, which means that the database is optimally designed to reduce redundancy and to improve the data integrity.

Ensuring Data Integrity

Data integrity refers to having correct or valid data in the database. You can address this in the design process by identifying how to restrict a user's ability to enter incorrect data. One way to ensure data integrity is to limit the type of allowable data entered in a field, which can be done by setting specific options in "Field Properties". You will learn about this in a future lesson, but remember data integrity should considered during the database design process.

Assume you are tasked with creating a database to track travel agency clients, their agents and the trips they have booked and will book with your firm. Determine the fields for each table using the database diagram below.

1.   **Based on the database structure below, identify the two "one to many" table relationships created. [Hints: Can an agent have more than one client? Can a client book more than one trip?]**

2.   **Based on the database structure below, how many fields are contained in each table? [Hint: The Agents table contains three fields.]**

3.   **For the number of fields contained in each table, determine what information should be contained in each field and name the fields. [Hints: Contact information for clients would be needed, as well as trip departure date, return date, and destination.]**

4.   **Enter the field names in each table. Be sure to consider how the tables link to each other.**

Note: The Primary Key is represented by a key symbol 🔑 .

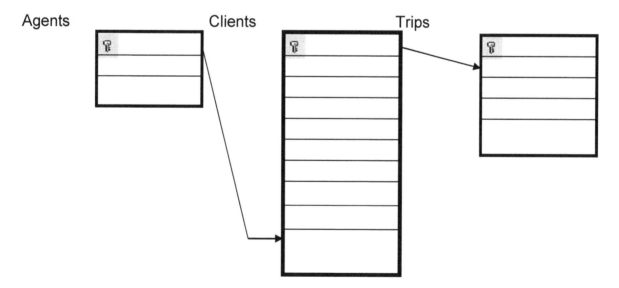

You will be working with a similar database in the remaining lessons. You can see how well you did designing the basic database structure in the next lesson.

Lesson #2: Creating a New Database

In this lesson you will learn to:

Create a Database File
Create Tables
Name and Describe Fields
Set a Primary Key

Lesson #2: Creating a new database

Creating the Access database file

Before you can create tables, you must create the Access file that will hold the database tables, forms, queries, and reports. You will use this file name to open the database when you wish to use it.

1. Start Microsoft Access.

You may start Access from either the Desktop or the Start menu. How you start Access depends on your computer.

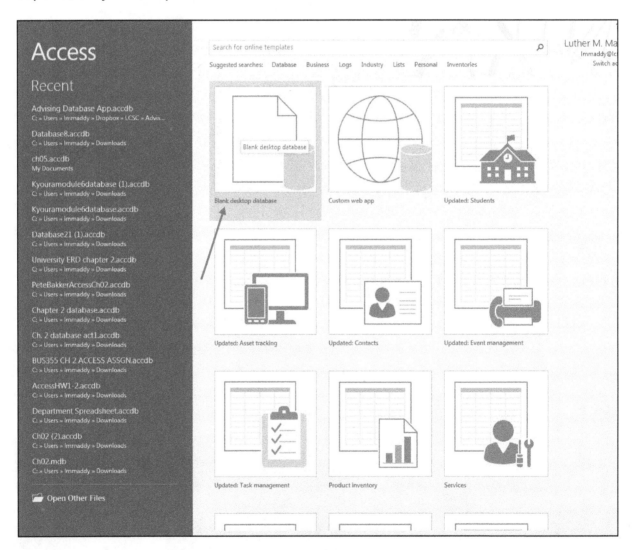

Each time you start Access you will see this screen, the Backstage view, which lets you open a new or existing database file. The default option (marked by the arrow above) is creating a new blank database. You can also open an existing database file using the menu on the left side.

When creating a new database, you can also select a premade database template on this screen. We will choose a blank database in this course, not only to learn the features of Access, but also because a custom designed database is tailored to your needs.

2.   Click Blank Desktop Database to create a new database.

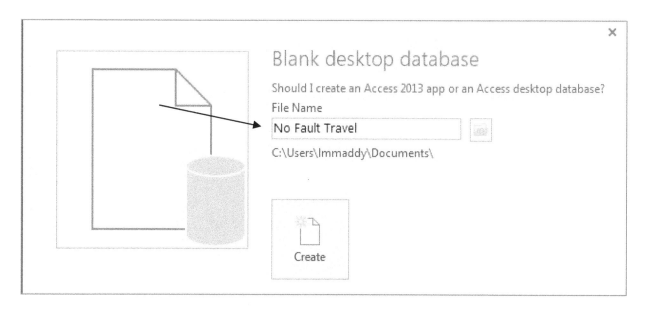

You will now be prompted to name the Access database file. A default location is selected, but you can also select its location.

1.   If needed, you can click the browse tool to store this file in another drive or folder. After selecting the desired folder, enter *No Fault Travel* as the file name and then click the Create button.

You have now created the Access file that will hold the tables and other objects of this database.

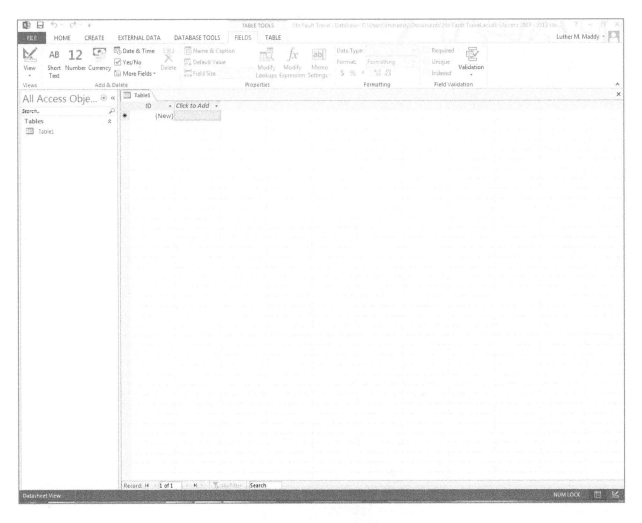

You will now create the first table for the No Fault Travel agency database.

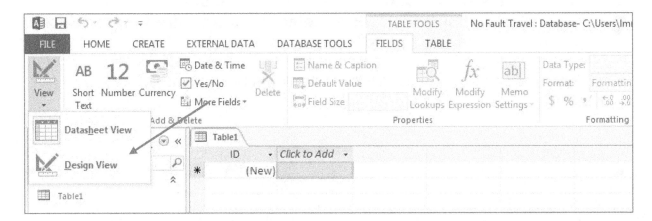

2.   In the Views group on the left side of the ribbon, click the View button to change the table view to Design View. (Note: You can also accomplish this by clicking on the drop-down arrow.)

The Save As dialog box appears. You will now name this table.

3.   Type *Travel Agents* in the text box and click OK.

Access has named this table *Travel Agents* and switched to Table Design view, which allows you to create or modify a table. You can specify the name, data type, and description for each field in a table using Table Design view. You can also set Field Properties, which you will learn about later in this course.

Field Names

Field names can be up to 64 characters long and consist of letters or numbers. Although spaces can be included in a field name, you should avoid them if you wish to later integrate your Access database with other database systems.

4.   Replace ID with *AgentID* as the name of the first field in this table and then press (Tab).

You are now in the Data Type column, where you can specify the type of information. When you create a new table, Access will name the first field ID and set it as the Primary Key. By default, the Data Type is set to Auto Number. If you would prefer another name for your first field, you can change it as you did here.

You will now view the different data types available in Access.

5.   In the Data Type column, click the drop-down list to display the various field types.

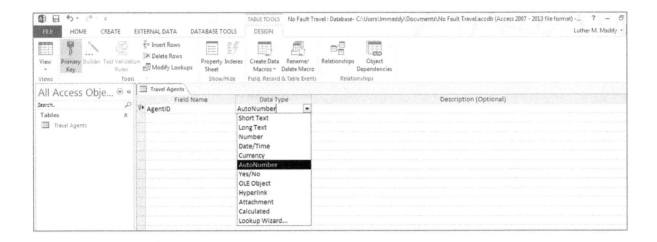

Field types

As you can see from the list, there are several field types. A definition of the field types is as follows:

Short Text: Short text fields hold alphanumeric information such as names and addresses. You should also use text fields to store numeric information that you will not use in calculations such as zip codes. Short Text fields can hold a maximum of 255 characters.

Long Text: Long text fields hold the same kind of information as short text fields. However, memo fields can store a maximum of 65,535 characters.

Number: Number fields hold numeric information that you intend to use in computations such as quantity or temperature.

Date/Time: Date/Time fields hold dates or times. You can view and enter this information in various formats. Storing dates and times in this field type also allows you to perform computations with your date and time data.

Currency: Currency fields hold numeric information. However, numbers stored in this field type will automatically be displayed in currency format ($33.44) for example. Currency fields would be used for fields like PayRate and Price.

AutoNumber: An Autonumber field type generates a unique sequentially increasing number for each new record. In tables created by default, the first field in a blank Access table is the primary key named ID of field type, AutoNumber. However, other fields containing unique information such as social security number can be used for the primary key and Autonumber is a useful field type to provide sequential numbers even when not used as a primary key.

Yes/No: Yes/No fields contain only the values Yes or No. Use this field type for enabling certain categories or answering simple yes or no questions. For example, a field named Active Customer would be a Yes/No field.

OLE Object: Use this field type when you want to store graphic information, such as a client's photograph.

Hyperlink: A hyperlink lets you store a link to something else. You could, for example, have a field named Vendor Web Site. Storing the vendor's Internet address in a Hyperlink field would enable you to quickly link to their site directly from Access. You can also use this field type to link to a document in Word or Excel.

Attachment: Attachment fields let you attach files such as pictures, documents, or spreadsheets to the record.

Calculated: Calculated fields allow you to perform computations based on other fields in the table.

6.   Choose AutoNumber as the data type for the AgentID field and press (Tab) to move to the Description column.

When choosing a data type, you can just type the first letter of the data type to move to that data type. Typing an "s" for example, moves to the Short Text type.

Field Descriptions

Field descriptions are optional. However, the text you type in this column will show up on the status bar at the bottom of the screen when you are in that field. The field description is a good way to inform users what the field's purpose is and how it works.

7.   In the field description for AgentID type: *Access will fill this value in for you* and then press (Enter).

You entered this description so users of this database will know they should not attempt to enter information into this field.

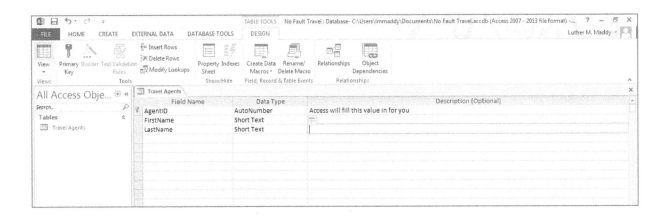

8.   Name the next two fields, *FirstName* and *LastName,* with Short Text as the data type and no descriptions.

Both of these fields will be short text fields. You do not need a description for these fields.

The first table for the No Fault travel agency is now complete. It has been constructed to store each travel agent's ID, first name, and last name.

Setting the Primary Key

As mentioned when discussing AutoNumber, Access automatically sets a primary key when it creates the first field in a new table. Although you can change the primary key to another field, using the first field in the table as the primary key is a good practice. You can set or unset a primary key by clicking Primary Key in the Tools group on the Table Tools Design tab.

Saving the Table

Now that you have added all the fields to this table, you are ready to save the table.

1.   Click the Save icon on the Quick Access bar.

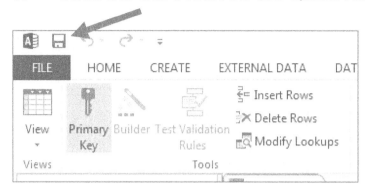

2.   In the Table Design window, click the small *x* in the top right-hand corner.

You are closing only the table. The Access database file will remain open.

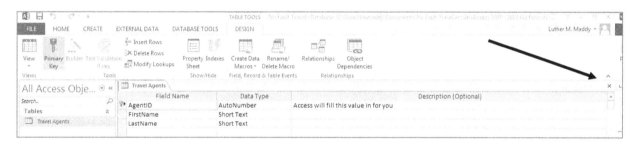

You should see Travel Agents in the list of tables in the All Access Objects navigation pane on the left. In the next steps, you will create two additional tables for the No Fault travel agency database.

First, you will create a table to store information about the travel agency's clients.

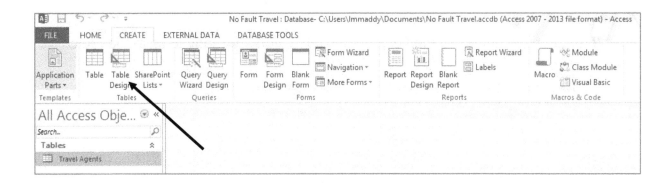

3.   Display the Create tab and click the Table Design tool in the Tables group.

You will be working in the Table Design View to create this table. Directly choosing to create a Table Design (instead of first creating a Table) saves the step of having to switch into Design View. Also note, when you create Table Design, rather than a Table, the first field is not automatically set as the primary key with field name *ID* of type AutoNumber.

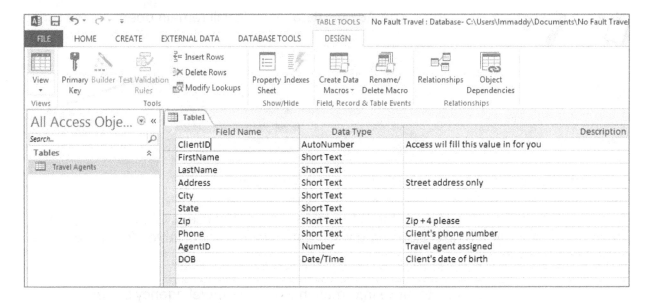

4.   Enter the field names, types and descriptions as shown. Be sure that the Data Type for the field *ClientID* is set to AutoNumber. Set the Data Types for the Fields *AgentID* and *DOB* to Number and Date/Time, respectively.

You will add formatting to these fields later too ensure consistency in the way users enter data, such as date of birth and phone number.

Note: To keep things simple, you created a single address field in our *Client* table. However, when creating tables to store personal contact information, you probably need two address fields, which could be named *Address1* and *Address2*.

Although Access does allow spaces in field names, learning not to use them is a good practice in the long run because some of Access's intermediate and advanced features are easier to use when spaces are not present. Furthermore, other database systems like SQL and MySQL do not allow the use of spaces in field names.

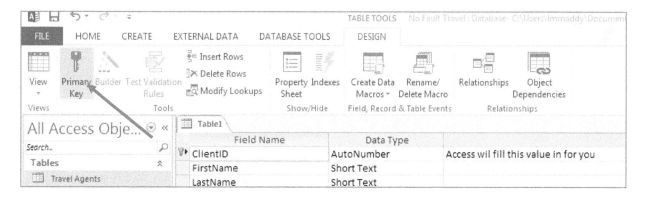

5.   Move into the ClientID field and click the Primary Key tool to set this field as the primary key.

6.   Save this table as *Clients* and then close it.

Notice that both the *Clients* and *Travel Agents* tables are visible in the Access navigation pane.

You will now create a third table to store the trips that clients have booked.

1.   On the Create tab, click the Table Design tool.

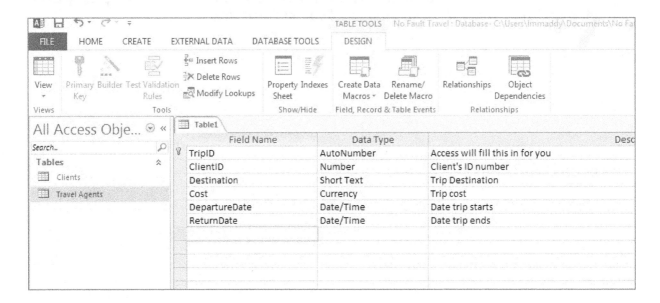

2.   Enter the field names, data types and descriptions as shown.

3.   Make the TripID field the Primary Key of this table.

To do this, move into the field and click the Primary Key tool on the ribbon.

4.   Save this table as *Trips* and then close it.

You now have three tables in this database file, *No Fault Travel*. These tables will hold the records you enter in this database. You will be adding additional database objects such as forms, queries, and reports as you continue the lessons in this workbook.

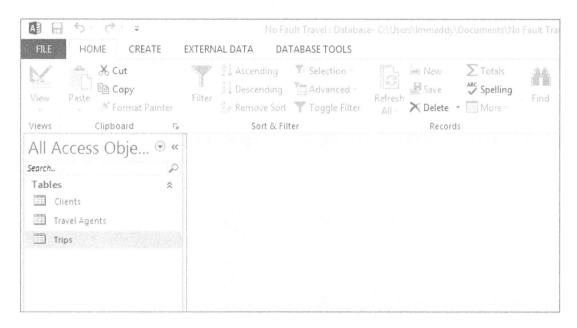

You will now close this database. In the following lesson skill builder, you will create a new database and two tables.

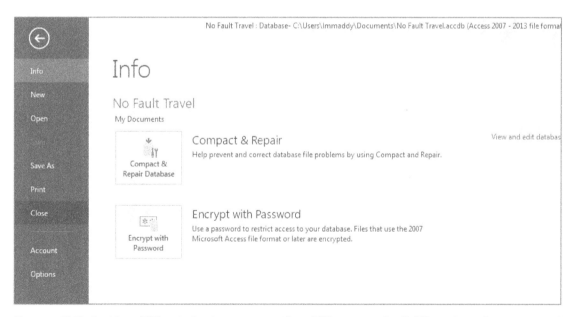

5. Click the File tab to open the Microsoft Office backstage view. Select Close to close the *No Fault Travel* Access file.

You have closed the database for the No Fault travel agency. Now you can create a new database or open an existing database.

Skill builder: Lesson #2

1. **Click the new Blank database tool to create a new database.**

2. **Name this database *Employees*.**

3. **In the *Employees* database, create a table named *Employees* with the following field names, data types and descriptions:**

	Name	Type	Description
Pri Key	EmployeeID	AutoNumber	Access will fill this value in for you
	Fname	Text	Employee's First name
	Lname	Text	Employee's Last name
	Address	Text	Street Address
	City	Text	
	State	Text	
	Zip	Text	
	DOH	Date/Time	Employee's Original Hire Date

4. **Create another table named *Positions* using the following field information:**

	Name	Type	Description
Pri Key	PositionID	AutoNumber	Access will fill this value in for you
	Title	Text	Employee's Job Title
	Department	Text	Employee's Department
	Supervisor	Text	Employee's supervisor
	DIP	Date/Time	Date Hired in Position
	PayRate	Currency	Employee's Hourly Rate
	EmployeeID	Number	Employee's ID number

5. **Close the database after saving both tables.**

Lesson #3: Creating Relationships

In this lesson you will learn to:

Create Relationships
Enforce Referential Integrity
Cascade Update
Cascade Delete

Lesson #3: Creating Relationships

Relating or linking tables allows you to share information between tables. In the *No Fault Travel* agency database you are building in the workbook lessons, you will link the *Travel Agents* table with the *Clients* table. You will also link the *Clients* and *Trips* tables. Relating, or normalizing tables, you should recall reduces data redundancy (which saves space) and improves data integrity. By linking the *Clients* table to the *Trips* table, only a field for the client's ID number needs to be included in the *Trips* table to link a trip with a client.

1.   Click the File tab to display the Backstage view. Choose Open.

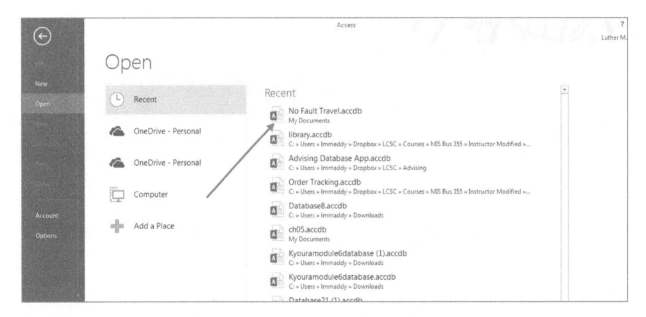

Access will display a list of files you have recently opened. In this case, the *No Fault Travel* database should be in this list. If not, you can use the Browse feature to find the location of the file.

2.   Click the No Fault Travel database file in the list of recent files to open it.

In the next steps, you will create the relationships you need in this database. Some features you use in Access will create links in tables. These features include queries and lookup fields. Creating your own links before you start using the database allows you to choose relationship options that Access does not automatically use. Creating relationships before adding data ensures that when data is added, it will follow the relationship rules you set up.

3.   Open the Database Tools tab, then choose Relationships.

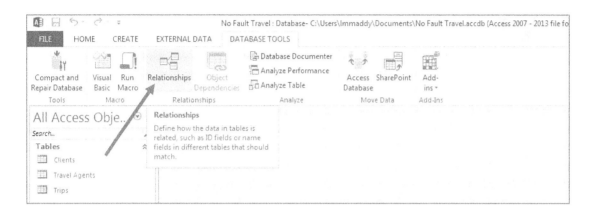

The Show Table dialog box appears where you choose the tables that you wish to relate. In this case, you will add all three tables.

4.   In the Show Table dialog box, select the *Travel Agents* table and click Add.

The *Travel Agents* table should now be displayed in the Relationships window. Move the Show Table dialog box below the area of the table information (by dragging its title bar down), so that the tables will not be covered by the Show Table dialog box.

5.   Select *Clients* and then click Add. Next, select Trips and click Add.

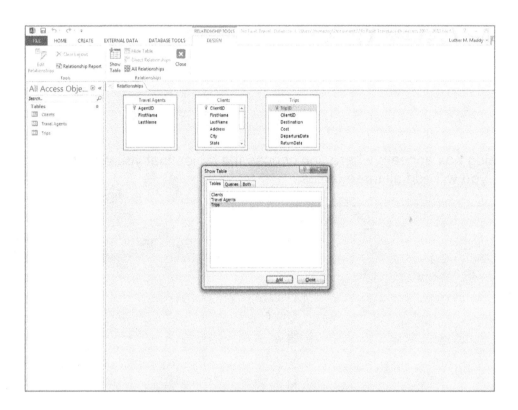

6.   After adding all three tables, click Close to close the Show Table dialog box.

You should now see all three tables in the Relationships window. If you inadvertently added a table more than once, you can click the title bar of the extra table and then press (Delete) to remove the extra occurrence of the table.

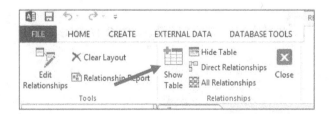

If you skipped a table, you can click the Show Table tool on the ribbon to open the Show Table dialog box. This will allow you to add the missing table or tables.

After adding all three tables you are now ready to create the relationships between them.

7.   Scroll down in the *Clients* table so that the AgentID field is visible in the field list.

The relationship you will create between the *Travel Agents* and *Clients* tables will be based on the *AgentID* field. This field is the primary key in the *Travel Agents* table. It is **not** the primary key in the *Clients* table. In the *Clients* table, it is called a foreign key.

If the *AgentID* field were the primary key in the *Clients* table and the *Agents* table, that would mean that each agent could have only one client. The relationship you are about to create is a one to many relationship, which means that one agent may have many clients.

8.   Carefully drag the *AgentID* field from the Travel Agents table and place it on top of the *AgentID* field in the Clients table.

The Edit Relationships dialog box should appear where you will specify the relationship options you want between these two tables.

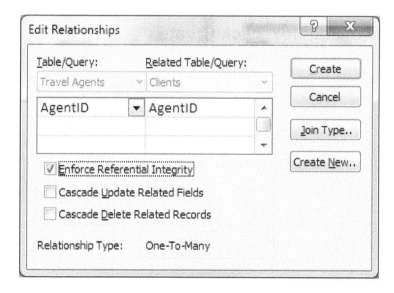

9.   In the Edit Relationships dialog box, turn on the Enforce Referential Integrity check box.

Enforce Referential Integrity

You have told Access to check the validity of the *AgentID* field when this value is entered into the *Clients* table. You will want to enable this option for most relationships you create. This check ensures that every client will be assigned a valid travel agent identification number. Otherwise, values might be permitted in this field that do not correspond to actual agents listed in the *Agents* table.

Cascade Update

When you selected Enforce Referential Integrity, the Cascade Update Related Fields option became available. Turning on this option allows you to change the travel agent's ID number in the *Travel Agents* table and have Access automatically change this value for all the clients assigned to this travel agent in the *Clients* table. This is an option you will want to enable in most of your databases; however, when using the AutoNumber field type for the primary key as we did in the *AgentID* field in the *Travel Agents* table, this option has no effect.

1.   **Turn the Cascade update option on.**

2.   **In the Edit Relationships dialog box, click Create.**

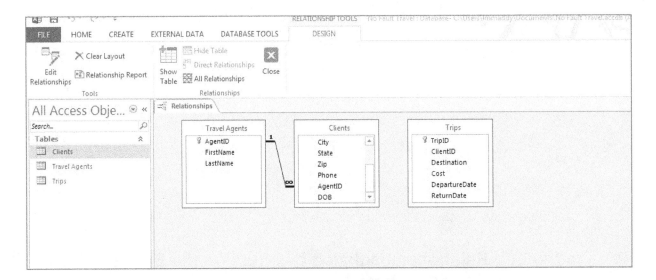

You should now see a join line between these two tables. You should also notice that Access has created a one to many relationship (i.e., one agent may have many clients).

3.   **Now, scroll up in the Clients table to display the *ClientID* field.**

4. **Drag the ClientID field from the Clients table and place it on top of the ClientID field in the Trips table.**

You should once again see the Edit Relationships dialog box.

5. **In the Edit Relationships dialog box, enable the Enforce Referential Integrity option.**

6. **Enable the Cascade Update Related Fields option.**

Cascade Delete

With this option enabled, if you delete a client from the database then all the trips booked for that client would also be deleted. This option causes the deletion of the "many" records associated with the "one" when the one record is deleted.

Use extreme care when determining if this option should be enabled! In our *No Fault Travel* database, this is an option you will enable. If you delete a client, you do not want the *Trips* table keep trip information without identifying who took those trips. If you delete a client, all the trips for that client should also be deleted. Of course, use caution any time you delete a record.

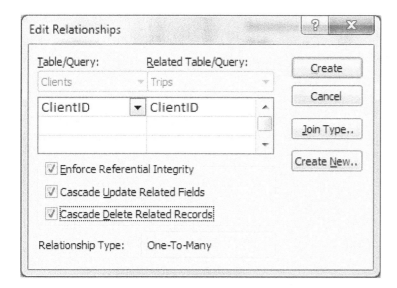

1. **Enable the Cascade Delete Related Records option in the Edit Relationships dialog box and click Create.**

You have now created a relationship between the *Clients* and *Trips* tables. You should see that this relationship is also "one to many." With this relationship, each client may book one or more trips.

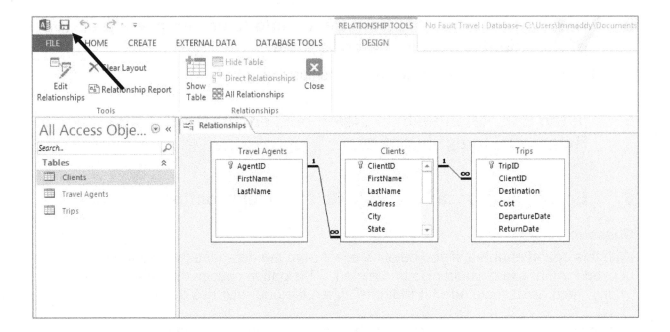

2.   On the Quick Access bar, click Save.

This saves the file with the new relationships.

3.   Close the Relationships window by clicking the Close button in the Relationships group.

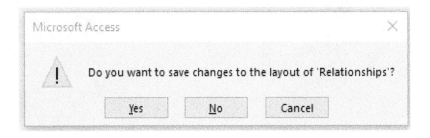

If you do not save before closing the relationships, Access will display the dialog box above.

4.   Close the No Fault Travel database.

Skill builder: Lesson #3

1.   Open the *Employees* database.

2.   Create a "one to many" relationship between the *Employees* and *Positions* tables based on the *EmployeeID* field. Select the options enforce referential integrity, cascade update related fields and cascade delete related related records.

3.   Save the relationship layout and close the database.

Lesson #4: Setting Field Properties

In this lesson you will learn to:

Modify table design
Set field properties
   Use Validation rules
   Set default values

Lesson #4: Setting Field Properties

Changing Table Design

Generally, you want to avoid changes in table design after you have created other Access objects such as queries, forms, and reports, which are developed from table contents. Since we have not created any other Access objects yet or entered data into our *No Fault Travel* agency database, a table design change at this point will not have any inconvenient or time consuming consequences.

When changing the design of tables, you can add, delete, or rename fields. Another very important aspect of table design addressed in this lesson is setting field properties. Field properties allow you to add restrictions to the values that can be entered into fields, and thereby help you maintain data integrity in the database.

In this exercise you will add a field and set field properties.

1.   Open the No Fault Travel database.

You will now enter the Design View of the *Clients* table, where you can make changes to the table's design.

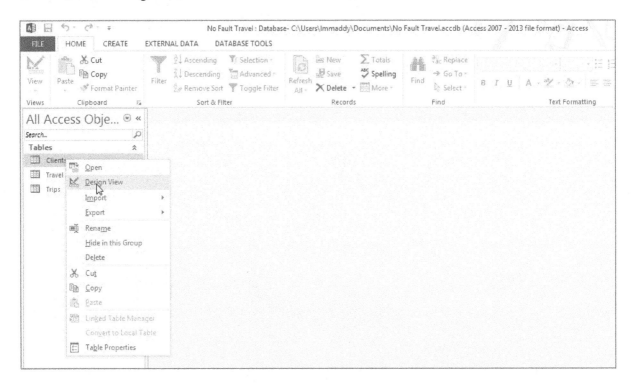

2.   In the list of tables, right-click *Clients* and then select Design View.

Inserting a field

To add a new field, move to a blank row after the last field name and type the name for the new field. If you wish to insert a row above an existing field, move to this field and right click the gray button (i.e., the field selector) just to the left of the field name. Then, from the shortcut menu, choose Insert Row.

1.   Right-click on the field selector for the DOB field (the box to the left of the field name).

The shortcut menu for the field should open.

2.   On the shortcut menu, select Insert Rows.

A new field should appear above the DOB field.

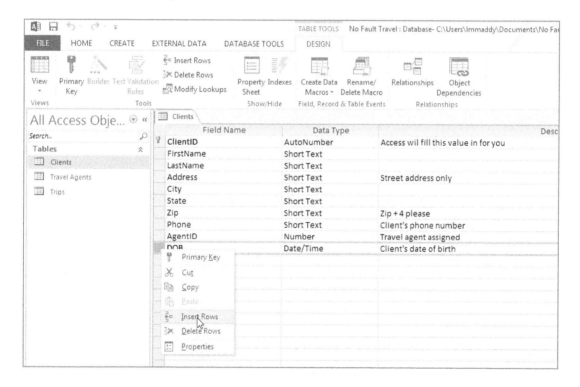

3.   Click in the Field Name cell for this new field and type *ActiveCustomer*.

4.   Choose Yes/No as the Data Type.

5.   In the Description column type, *Choose 'Yes' if this is an active customer.*

Using a field with this data type allows you to easily specify if a customer is active or inactive. Including this field is useful because it allows you to view only active clients, or create reports which list only active or inactive clients.

6.   Save the table after making these changes, but stay in Design View.

Setting Field Properties

You will now set some field properties in this table to have some control on the values entered in those fields. Notice the Field Properties section in the lower portion of the Design View window. Here you can view or make changes to a field's properties.

1.   Move up to and click in the *FirstName* field.

Look at the Field Properties for the FirstName field. Notice the Field Size is 255.

General	Lookup
Field Size	255
Format	
Input Mask	
Caption	
Default Value	
Validation Rule	
Validation Text	
Required	No
Allow Zero Length	Yes
Indexed	No
Unicode Compression	Yes
IME Mode	No Control
IME Sentence Mode	None
Text Align	General

The Field Size Property

By default, Access sets all short text fields to 255 characters, the maximum size of short text. You will want to reduce the field size when fewer characters are needed.

For example, if you need 6 characters in a field, a field size of 255 characters increases the chances of data error. When determining the field size setting, it is better to start too small and increase the field size, rather than to start too large and shrink the field. If you reduce the field size after entering data, you run the risk of truncating some data by making the field smaller than the size of previously entered data.

2.   Move the mouse to Field Size in the Field Properties of the *FirstName* field. Change the Field Size to 12 characters.

3.   Change the Field Size of the following fields as indicated:

LastName	20
Address	30
City	15
State	2
Zip	10
Phone	14

You only want to change the field size of the fields with the data type short text in this table. Leave the fields with other data types as they are for right now.

Format Property

Some field data types, such as Date/Time and Number, allow you to specify how you would like the data to appear in those fields. You can choose from several different formats for date fields. Access can display the month name or use numbers for the entire date. The format property allows you to choose from the available options. When you click Format under General Field Property, Access will display a drop-down arrow, which when clicked provides list of choices.

The format property for text fields does not offer a drop-down list of formatting options. However, text fields will be displayed in all uppercase or lowercase format if you enter a greater than (>) or a less than (<) symbol, respectively, as the field property for Format.

1.   Move to the DOB field. Then move to Format under the Field Properties for the DOB field and click the drop-down list arrow.

2.   From the list of Date/Time formats, choose Short Date.

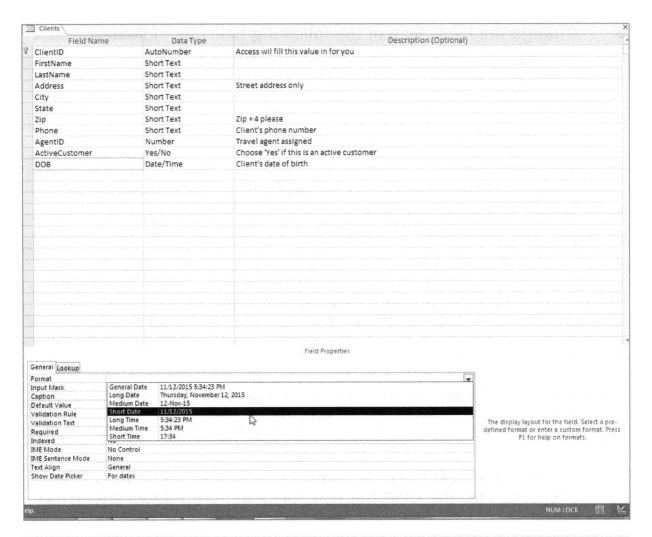

Using Input Masks

Input masks can make data input quicker and easier by having Access automatically provide formatting features such as slashes (/) in dates and other formatting options. Input masks also help control the kind of data than can be entered into fields.

When working with dates, century compliance is a concern. If the date field will contain dates before 1930, it will be necessary for the user to input the complete four digit year, such as 1922. Otherwise, Access will assume the century is 2000 rather than 1900.

With our *No Fault Travel* agency database, the DOB field of the *Clients* table could contain dates prior to 1930. By entering the correct input mask you can require that every date entered here have all four digits for the year.

1. **Click in the Input Mask row for the DOB field. Click the button with three dots on the right …. In the Input Mask dialog box, choose Short Date, and click Next. The default input mask is 99/99/0000, click Next, and then press (Enter).**

The "0000" in the input mask will require that all dates entered into this field have all four digits for the year.

2. **Save the *Clients* table but stay in Design View.**

Using the Input Mask Wizard

As you just saw, Access provides a wizard to assist in creating input masks. In this portion of this lesson you will use the Input Mask Wizard to create input masks for the phone number and zip code fields.

1. Move into the Zip field.

2. Click in the Input Mask row under the General Field Properties of the *Zip* field.

If Access asks you to save the table, answer Yes.

3. In the Input Mask row, click the "build" ⬜ on the right.

The Input Mask Wizard should open to lead you through the creation of this input mask.

If Access asks you to save the table, answer Yes.

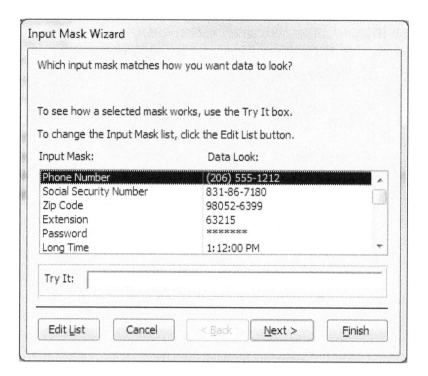

2.   In the Input Mask dialog box, select Zip Code and click Next.

3.   **In the next step in the Input Mask Wizard, a nine-digit zip code format is the default provided (with a hyphen to separate the four extension digits). Click Next again.**

The input mask uses both zeroes and nines. The zeros are required input for the five-digit zip code. The nines indicate that the four extension digits are optional. If you want to require all nine digits, change the nines to zeroes in the input mask.

5.   **Select the option to store the data with symbols in the mask, and click Next.**

Here you have told Access to store the hyphen (-) in the zip code so that it displays correctly in reports and labels.

6.   **Click Finish on the final Input Mask Wizard dialog box.**

The input mask you just created should appear in the Input Mask row under General Field Properties of the *Zip* field in the *Clients* table.

7. **Save the table to keep this change.**

8. **Move into the _Phone_ field, so that the Field Properties for _Phone_ become accessible. Now click in the Input Mask row under General Field Properties.**

9. **Use the Input Mask wizard to build an input mask for the _Phone_ field. Accept the default options for the data look and the input mask, (999) 000-000. However, be sure to store the data with the symbols in the mask (e.g., (976) 472-3491).**

The Field Properties for the _Phone_ field should now appear as above with the input mask created by the wizard in the Input Mask row.

Validation Rules

Validation rules let you restrict the information or values that can be entered into a field. Applying validation rules helps ensure data integrity and can make data entry easier. In the next steps, you will apply a data validation rule to the *State* field.

1. **Move into the State Field and add the description:** *Only CA, ID, OR, and WA are allowed.*

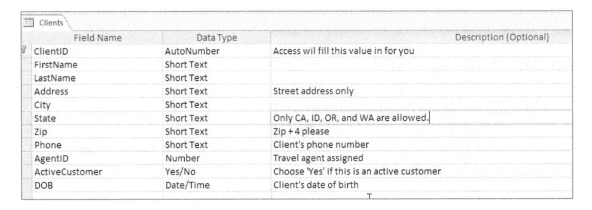

This description will be visible to the person entering data in the table. However, the description only makes a suggestion to the user to enter those four states into the *State* field; it does not prevent other states from being entered.

You will create a validation rule that will only allow the four states to be entered into the *State* field.

2. **Move into the State field. Now, click in the Validation Rule row in the Field Properties section.**

3. **Type** *CA or ID or OR or WA* **and press (Enter).**

You can see that Access added quotation marks, such as "CA", around the abbreviation for each state. Access will not allow any values other than what you typed into this field.

Validation Text

After entering a validation rule, Access will not allow any data that does not match the value(s) specified by you. If a user attempts to input incorrect data, Access will display a default error message stating that the data does not meet the validation rule. You can also replace the default message by a user-friendly one in the Validation Text property.

4. Move to the Validation Text property of the *State* field and type *The client must live in CA, ID, OR, or WA. No other states are allowed.*

Access will now display this message when incorrect data is entered into the State field.

Default Values

If the user will repeatedly enter the same value in a record field, you can have Access automatically enter that as the default value in new records. Of course, the default value can be changed by the user. In the next steps, you will add default values for the *State* and *ActiveCustomer* fields.

1. Move to the Default Value row of the *State* field. Type *ID* and then press (Enter).

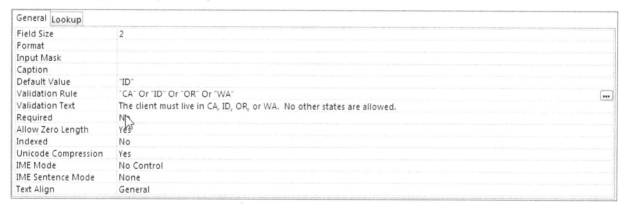

General	Lookup	
Field Size	2	
Format		
Input Mask		
Caption		
Default Value	"ID"	
Validation Rule	"CA" Or "ID" Or "OR" Or "WA"	...
Validation Text	The client must live in CA, ID, OR, or WA. No other states are allowed.	
Required	No	
Allow Zero Length	Yes	
Indexed	No	
Unicode Compression	Yes	
IME Mode	No Control	
IME Sentence Mode	None	
Text Align	General	

Access adds the quotation marks for you.

2. Move to the Format row and insert the greater than symbol (>).

Access will display the state abbreviations in upper case letters, even if the user entered any part of the state abbreviation in lower case.

3. **Now move to the *ActiveCustomer* field so that its field properties are accessible. Type *Yes* in the Default Value row.**

Since most new customers will be "Active", you changed the default value of this field to Yes instead of No.

4. **Save and close the Clients table.**

5. **Enter the Design View of the Travel Agents table.**

You probably did this by double clicking on the table in the "All Access Objects" pane, and then selecting Design View from the View Group on the Home tab. However, remember you can also simply right click the table in the pane, and then select Design View from the shortcut menu options.

6. **Change the Field Size properties of the *FirstName* field to 12 and the *LastName* field to 20.**

7. **Save and close the Travel Agents table.**

8. **Enter the Design View of the Trips table.**

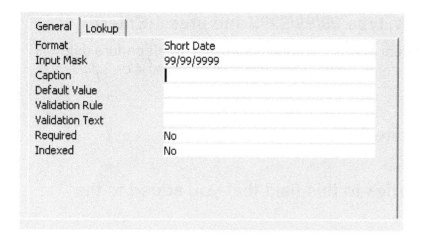

9.   Move to the DepartureDate field.

10.   Change the Format property to Short Date.

11. **In the Input Mask row, type *99/99/9999* and press (Enter).**

This time you used 9999 in the year instead of 0000 because a trip departure date will not be before 1930. A user may enter the year into this field as either 4 or 2 digits (i.e., 2017 or 17).

12. **Move to the ReturnDate field.**

13. **Add the same properties to this field that you added to the DepartureDate field.**

14. **Save and close the Trips table.**

15. **Close the No Fault Travel database.**

Skill builder: Lesson #4

1.   **Open the *Employees* database.**

2.   In the Employees table, change the format of the DOH field to Short Date and add the appropriate input mask.

3.   **In the *Positions* table, change the Field Size property of the Department field to 5.**

4.   **Add a validation rule to the *Department* field to only allow the departments of Admin, Sales or IT.**

5.   **Add an appropriate validation text message to the *Department* field.**

6.   **Change the formatting of the *DIP* field to short date and add the appropriate input mask.**

7.   **Close the database when done.**

Lesson #5: Working with Data in Tables

In this lesson you will learn to:

Enter Data
Edit Data
Sort Data
Delete Records

Lesson #5: Working with Data in Tables

1.   Open the No Fault Travel database.

2.   In the list of tables, right-click the *Travel Agents* table and then select Open on the shortcut menu.

You could also double-click the table to open it.

You should now see the Datasheet View of the table. In this lesson you will enter data directly into the table and then arrange the data using Datasheet View. In the next lesson you will create forms, which is a better way of viewing and entering data.

3.   Click in the *FirstName* field and type *Adam* and press (Tab).

As soon as you began typing the first name, Access entered a number in the AgentID field.

4.   In the *LastName* field type *Johnson* and press (Tab) twice.

Since Access will automatically enter the data in the *AgentID* field (because it has an AutoNumber field type), you skipped this field.

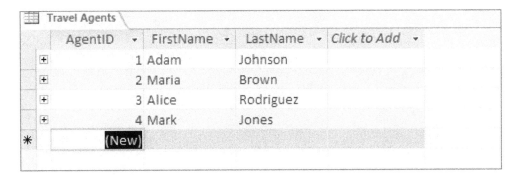

5.   Enter the additional records as shown above.

Sorting Table Data

By default, Access sorts the records in a table by the primary key. In this table the primary key, the *AgentID* field, has the field type AutoNumber, so the ascending successive order from 1 to 4 is the order in which the records were entered. You can easily change the sorting order using the sorting tools .

To change the sort order of a table, move into the field you want to sort on, and then click either Ascending or Descending tool in the Sort & Filter group on the Home tab ribbon.

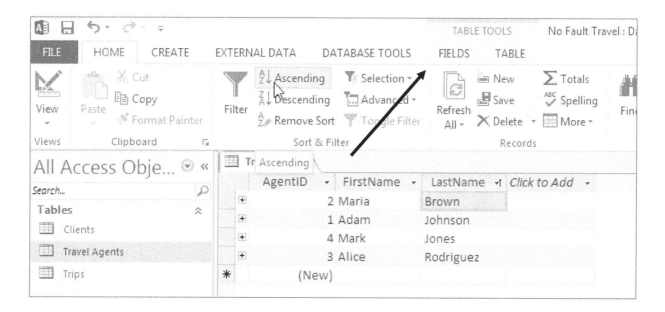

1.   **Click in any cell of the *LastName* field in the table. Then click the Ascending tool in the Sort & Filter group on the Home tab ribbon.**

The table is now sorted by last name.

Changing Column Widths

When you view data in a table, you may wish to adjust the width of a displayed column. Access allows you to increase or decrease a column width as desired.

To manually adjust the column width, move the mouse pointer to the right border of the heading of the column you want to adjust. When the mouse pointer turns into a "black crosshair," drag left to decrease the column width or drag right to increase column width.

To automatically adjust the column width, move the mouse pointer to the right border of the column heading you want to adjust. When the mouse pointer turns into the "black crosshair," double-click and the column wide will automatically adjust so that the largest entry (including field name) in that field is visible.

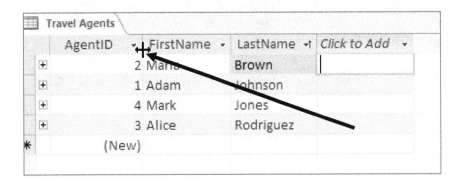

1.   **Move the mouse pointer between the *AgentID* and *FirstName* column headings and double-click.**

You should notice that Access decreased the width of the *AgentID* field column.

2.   **Use the same method to adjust the widths of the *FirstName* and *LastName* fields.**

3.   **Close the table.**

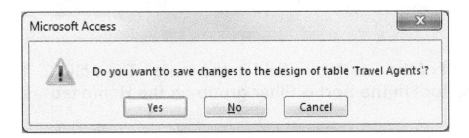

Access will ask if you want to save the changes you made to the design of this table. If you answer yes, the next time you open the table, it will be sorted by agent's last name and the column widths will be as they are now. If you answer no, the table will revert to the default design which you altered.

4.   **Click Yes to save the changes you just made to the table design.**

Editing Data

At some point, you will need to edit some data in the database. In the next steps, you will edit existing data from Datasheet View, but the same techniques can be used in forms.

1.   Open the *Travel Agents* table.

To open a table in Datasheet View, you can double-click it in the Objects pane.

2.   Double-click on Maria Brown's last name.

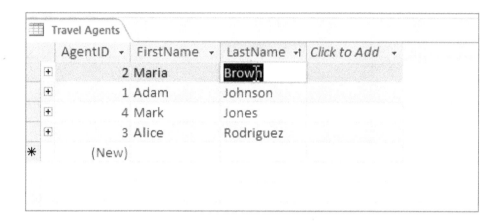

3.   Type *Green* and press (Enter).

When the entire contents of the field is selected, whatever you type replaces the entire contents in the field.

4.   Click the Undo tool on the Quick Access Toolbar to undo this change.

5.   Click to the right of Brown in Maria Brown's last name.

Notice that the insertion point is displayed. By single clicking in the cell, you can edit the cell contents letter by letter.

6.   Type an *e* and press (Enter) to change the spelling of Maria's last name.

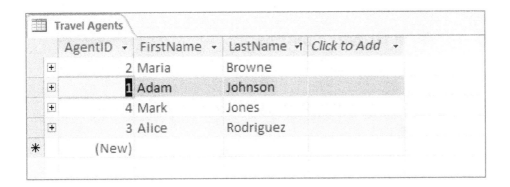

Deleting Records

Access helps safeguard from deleting records accidentally by requiring you to confirm that you want to delete a record. To delete a record, move into any cell in the row and click the Delete drop-down arrow in the Records group of the Home tab ribbon. On the Delete drop-down list, choose Delete Record. You will be asked if you are sure you want to delete the record. If you answer yes, you will never see that record again. Delete with care.

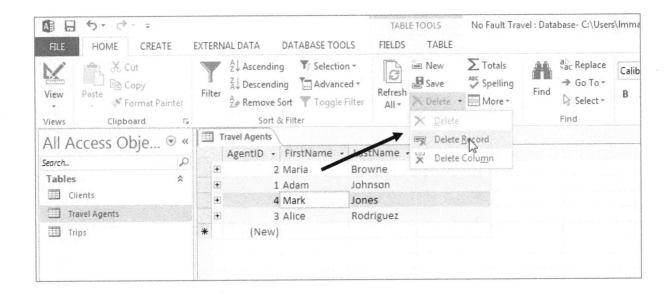

1.   **Move into Mark Jones' record and choose Delete Record from the Delete drop-down list.**

You will now see the delete confirmation.

2.   **Click Yes to delete the record.**

3.   **Close the *Travel Agents* table and the *No Fault Travel* database.**

Skill builder: Lesson #5

1.   Open the *Employee* database.

2.   Open the *Employees* table and enter the following record:

Fname	Andrew
Lname	Jackson
Address	833 Overland Rd.
City	Boise
State	ID
Zip	87704
DOH	09/22/07

3.   **Sort the table by employee's last name.**

You won't notice a difference now, but you will after you add additional records.

4.   **Have Access automatically (i.e., double-click) adjust the widths of all the columns.**

5.   **Close the table, answering Yes when asked if you want to save changes in the table design.**

6.   **Close the Employee database.**

Lesson #6: Creating and using forms

In this lesson you will learn to:

Use the Form Wizard
Use AutoForm
Modify Form Design
Enter Data in a Form
Use the Find Command

Lesson #6: Creating and Using Forms

Forms allow you to enter, edit, and view data. You can create a form that is identical to a form you are already using. Because you can customize form layout, forms also allow you to see record fields which may not be viewable from table Datasheet View in one screen width. Forms are very easy to create and use.

1.　Open the No Fault Travel database.

2.　Click the Create tab.

Currently, there are no forms in this database.

3.　Click Form Wizard from the Forms group.

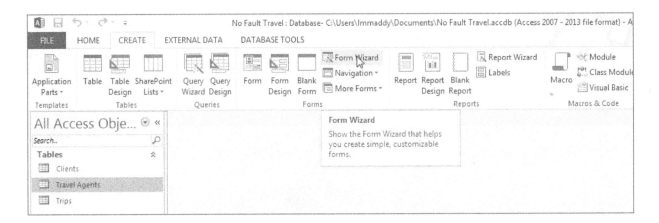

Using the Form Wizard

Using the Form Wizard, Access creates a form based on the choices you make. You decide on the basic layout, which fields you want to display, and the background style.

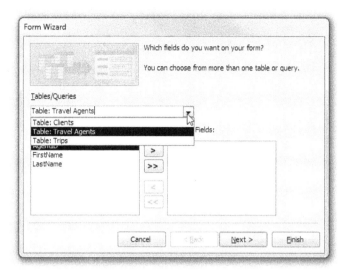

4. **Click the drop-down arrow under Tables/Queries, choose *Table: Travel Agents* from the selections provided.**

Next, you need to select which fields you want on the form in the order you want to see them.

5. **Click the** 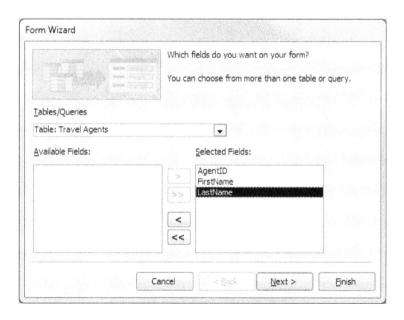 **button to add all the fields.**

Use the `>` button, if you want to add one field at a time. The buttons with the left pointing arrows similarly will remove the selected fields all at once or one at a time.

6.   After selecting all the fields, click Next to continue.

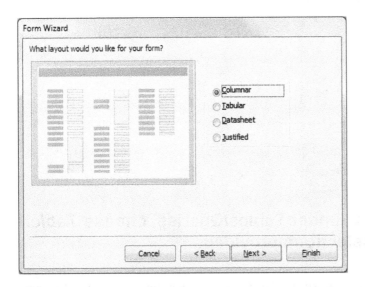

7.   Choose Columnar as the layout for this form and click Next.

Access will layout the form in columns.

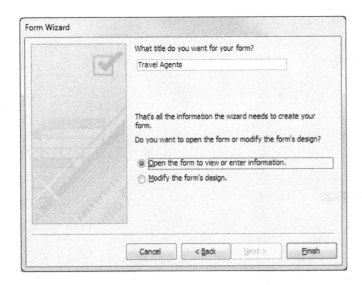

8.   If needed, type *Travel Agents* in the text box for the form title and click Finish.

You should now see the form you created using the Form Wizard.

Now, we will use the Design View of the form to change its appearance.

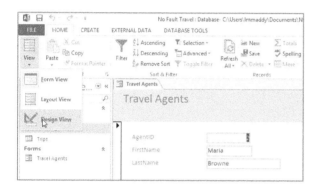

1.   In the Views group on the Home tab, click the View drop-down arrow. Choose Design View.

In Design View you can adjust the size of fields, add fields, or change the layout of the form. In this portion of the exercise you will adjust the size of the fields as they are displayed on the form.

2.   Click the AgentID textbox. Move the mouse pointer to the right edge. When you see the sizing arrow, drag left to decrease the size of this field.

Although it is not necessary, it is a good practice to leave the text box large enough so that the field name is visible when using Design View. The field name identifies the text box and makes future editing of the form easier.

3.   Adjust the text box sizes for the other fields on the form so that their widths appear similar those in the image below.

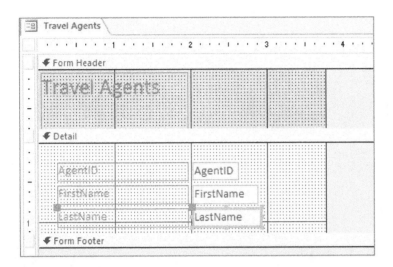

If you find at a later time that your field width is not large enough, you can re-enter the Design View of this form and increase the size of the field displayed.

4.   Save and close the form.

You should see the *Travel Agents* form listed under Forms in the All Access Objects pane on the left side of the screen.

Creating a Form using Form Design

The Form Wizard is a quick way to easily create form. But to modify the form, you need to use the Design View. In this portion of the lesson, you will create an entire form in Design View to help you learn more about forms and how to modify a form layout.

You will not create a Client entry/edit form that will resemble a paper form.

1.   Click the Create tab, then the Form Design tool in the Forms group on the ribbon.

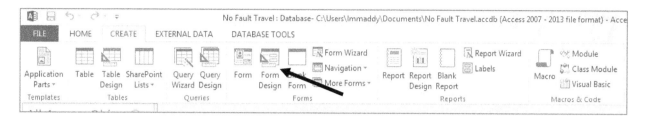

You are now in the form design view. You have a blank form and will layout the form one field at a time, exactly as you want the fields to appear.

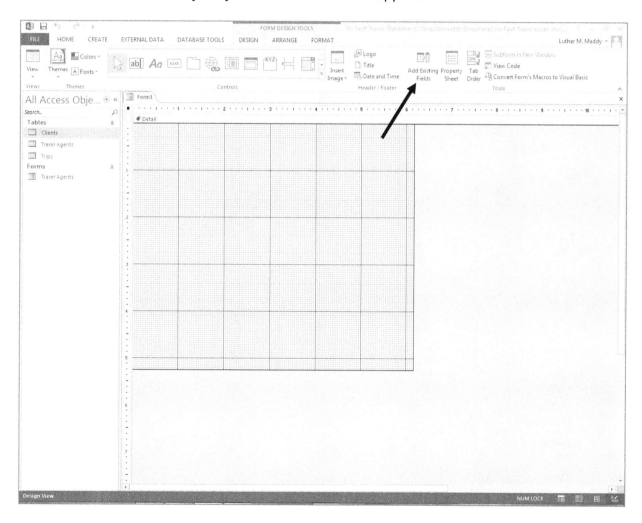

2. **Click the Form Design Tools Design tab. In the Tools group, click the Add Existing Fields tool.**

You will need to specify for which table you wish to use this form before you select the fields you want included on the form.

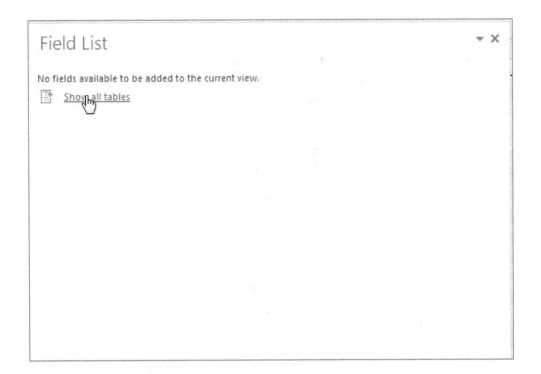

3.   In the Field List dialog box, click Show all tables.

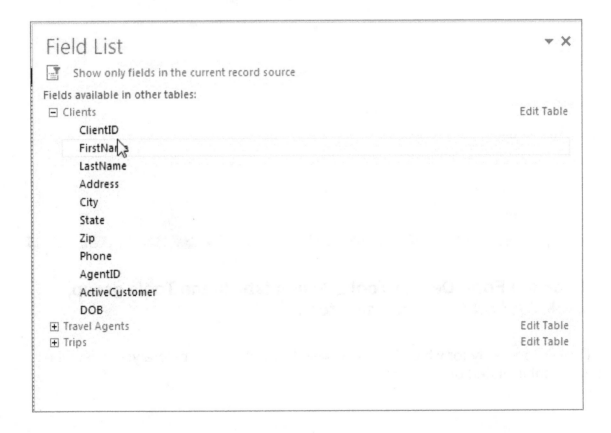

4. **Expand the *Clients* field list to view all fields by clicking the ⊞ to the left of Clients. Next, drag the *ClientID* field onto the form as shown.**

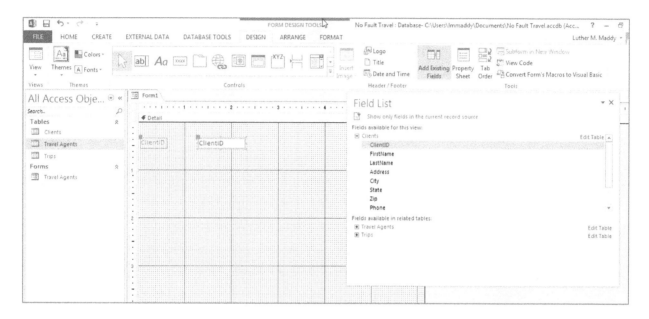

When you drag a field onto the form, Access places two controls with the same name on the form. The gray control is the label, the name of the field. You will not alter the field label when you enter or edit data on the form. However, you can edit the field label in Design View, so that the label displays other information to the form user, besides the field name.

The second control is the field text box, which holds the field information in the table. You can use the text box to enter or edit data. You do not want to edit the field name in the text box control when you are designing a form because that would break the link between the control on the form and the table field with the same name.

When you drag a field, Access places the top left edge of the field's text box at the mouse pointer's location. Access automatically places the label to the left.

You can move and size both the field label and text box, as you did previously. The text box and label are linked. If you move one, the other also moves unless you drag the top left corner of the field label or text box.

Tab Order on a Form

When using an Access form, you can move from field to field by pressing the (Tab) key. The tab order is defined by the order in which you dragged the fields onto the form. If you drag *ClientID* to the form first; Access assigns it the first tab stop. If *DOB* is the last field dragged to the form, Access will assign it as the last tab stop, no matter where it is placed on the form.

5.   Continue adding fields to the form so that it appears similar to the image below.

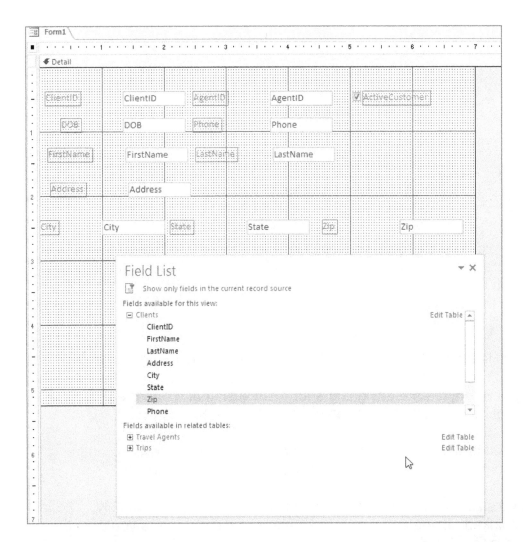

You can drag the field list to another location on the screen if needed. You can also move the fields in an attempt to properly align them. You will learn a better way to align fields later in this lesson.

6.   Close the Field list. Save the form as *Client Entry/Edit Form*, but leave it open and in Design view.

Modifying the Form's Design

After you create the basic form layout, you can move and size fields. In this portion of the exercise you will re-design this form.

Selecting Controls

You must select a control before you can move or size it. To select a control, just click it, and eight sizing handles (gold squares) will appear at the corners and midpoints on the box sides.

To select multiple controls, press and hold the shift key as you select each control. Each selected control will have sizing handles.

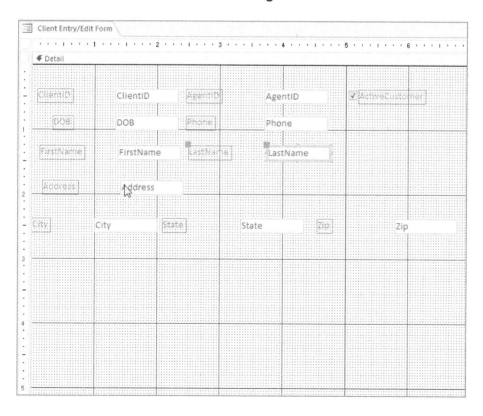

1.   **Click on the text box for the *LastName* field.**

The text box is the white box which in Form View you will see the actual data in the field. The label control is the gray box which displays the field name

Moving and sizing controls

When you selected the text box for the *LastName* field, the associated field label was also automatically selected. Whether you move one or both controls (i.e., field text box and label), or just size the selected control (in this case the text box) depends upon the shape of your mouse pointer when you drag.

 The "four-headed arrow" will move all selected controls. You will find this control when you point to any edge on the selected control, not near a sizing handle. (Reminder: If you point to the top left corner of a control, only that control will move.)

The "double-headed arrow" lets you size the control. The arrow direction indicates the direction of expansion -- vertically, horizontally, or diagonally as the example arrow here. The arrow direction depends on which sizing handle you are pointing to.

2.   **Move the mouse pointer to the sizing handle on the right side of the *LastName* field text box. A horizontal double-arrow should appear.**

3.   **Carefully drag the double-arrow right to increase the width of the text box by approximately ½ inch.**

This will allow space for longer last names.

4.   **Click the *State* field label (i.e., control) to select it.**

The field label is the control to the left of the field text box (also a control).

5.   **Move the mouse pointer to the top left corner of the *State* label control. This is referred to as the "move handle".**

You should see a four-headed arrow, which indicates you can move this control. Dragging from the top left corner allows you to move just that control, and not its associated control (in this case, the *State* field text box). Otherwise, the four-headed arrow would move both controls.

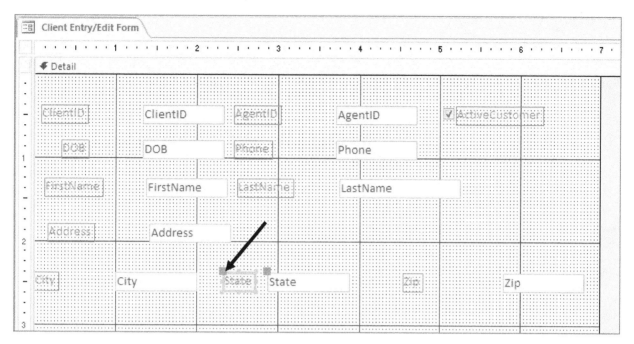

6.   Drag the *State* label control left so that it is closer to the *State* text box as shown.

7.   Now, repeat the moving and sizing methods to move and resize labels and text boxes to create a form similar to the one shown below.

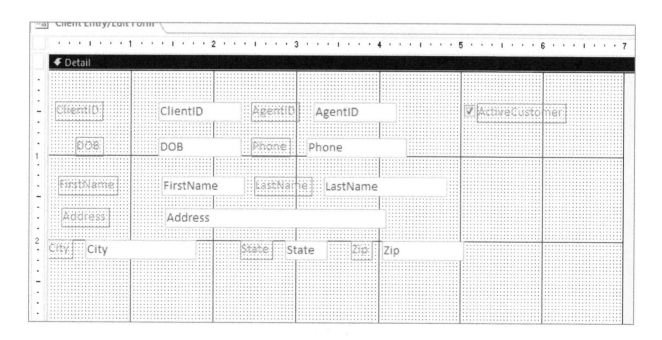

Entering Data in a Form

When you enter data into a form, press (Tab) or (Enter) to move to the next field. If you want to move to a previous field, press (Shift+Tab). After you have entered data in the last field and press (Tab) or (Enter), Access will display a new record for you to fill in.

1. **Click the Save tool on the Quick Access toolbar to save database with the modified form design.**

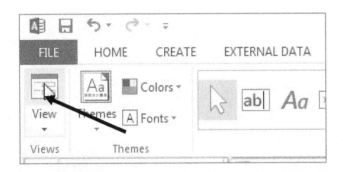

2. **In the View group on the Design tab, click the View drop-down arrow and select Form view.**

You have left design mode and can now work with the data. Notice you are working under the Home tab ribbon.

3. **Enter the data in the form as shown.**

Remember to skip over (i.e., just press Tab) the *ClientID* field.

4. **Press (Tab) after entering the last field, the zip code. Then, press (Page Up) to view the previous record (which you just entered).**

5. **On the Home tab ribbon, click the New tool in the Records group.**

6. **Enter the following data for three additional records:**

AgentID	2	1	1
FirstName:	Becky	Alvin	Robert
LastName	Adams	Black	Jones
Address	203 Pinewood	88 Fern	22 Oakridge
City	Boise	Caldwell	Nyssa
State	ID	ID	OR
Zip	83441	83655	85112
Active	YES	YES	NO
Date of Birth	5/17/1959	6/24/1972	8/15/1940
Phone	(208) 222-3433	(208) 443-6664	(541) 344-4455

The Record Navigation Bar

You can use the record navigation bar at the bottom of your form window to move easily from record to record. The two left buttons move to the first record (◄) or the previous record (◄). The first two right buttons move to the next record (►) or the last record (►►). The third right button (►) creates a new record.

7. **After entering these records, use the record navigation bar to go to the first record and then the last record.**

8. **In the last record, change the state to *UT* and press (Enter).**

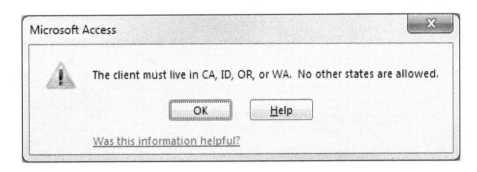

A Microsoft Access validation error message should appear and inform you that this is not a valid state.

9. **Click OK on the error message box. Then press (Esc) to return to the original data entered.**

10. **Close the Clients form. Answer "Yes" if asked to save the form.**

You will now create a tabular form based on the Trips table.

1. **Click the Create tab, and click the Form Wizard tool in the Forms group. Choose the *Trips* table and select all the fields in this table (>>), and then click Next.**

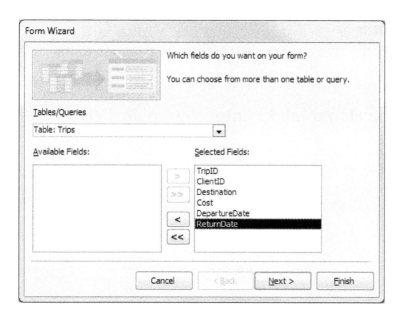

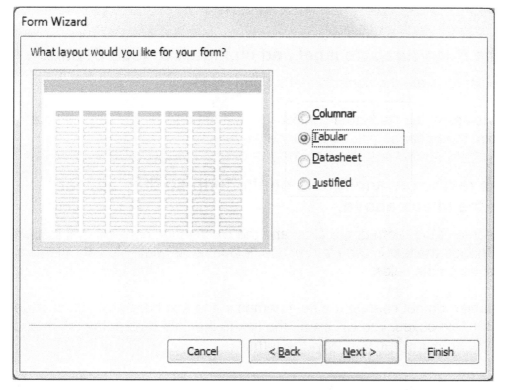

2.   Choose Tabular as the layout and click Next.

3.   Title the form _Trips Entry/Edit_ and click Finish.

Editing a Columnar or Tabular Form

In this portion of the lesson you will enter the design view and make changes to the form's design.

1. Use the View tool on the Home tab to enter the Design View.

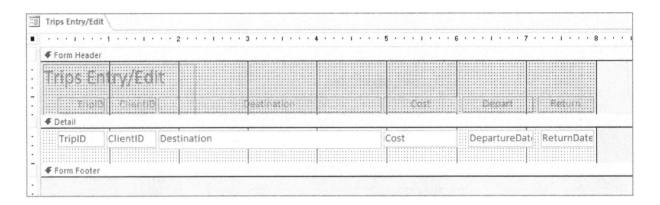

2. Click in the *DepartureDate* label and change it to read *Depart.*

The labels in a tabular form are the controls in the Form Header.

After clicking once to select the field label control, you will need to click a second time for the insertion point to appear so you can change the text.

3. Modify the textboxes and labels on the form so they appear similar to the image above.

You will need to decrease the width of the *Cost* and the *Destination* controls (field labels and text boxes). Change the text in the *ReturnDate* field label as well. You should also increase the size of both date fields.

As we discussed earlier, do not change the field names in the text boxes. If you change the field names in the text boxes, you will break the link to the field data in the table, and an error message will appear when you view the form.

The Center tool ($\equiv$) can be accessed from the Text Formatting group on the Home tab on the ribbon. You can use it to center the text in the labels on the Form Header.

4. Save the modified form.

5. Display this form in Form View and enter the records as shown below:

Note: For trips with *TripID* 3, 4, or 5, enter a departure date one day after today's date. Enter a return date 10 days after today's date.

The Ditto Command

When you are entering several values that are the same in different records, you may use the ditto command. Moving to the field you want to enter duplicate information in and pressing (Control+apostrophe) will cause the field information from the previous record to appear in the current record.

6. Close the form when done.

The Find command

You can use the Find command to quickly locate a particular record. The first step is to move into the field you wish to search. Then, select the Find command and specify the value you want to find in that field. To find specific records in large files, choose your search value carefully. Using the record's Primary Key as your search value is one way to ensure that you will quickly find the specific record you are seeking.

1. Open the Client Entry/Edit form.

Access will display the first record in the table. By default, the records are sorted by the Primary Key value.

2.   Press (Tab) until you move into the Last Name field.

In this exercise, you will search for a value in the *LastName* field.

3.   In the Find group on the Home tab ribbon, click the Find tool.

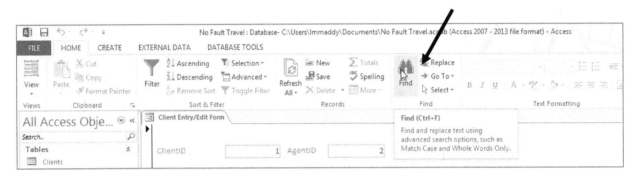

The Find and Replace dialog box should appear.

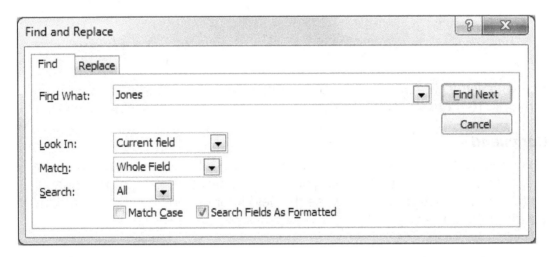

4.   In the Find What text box type *Jones,* and then click the Find Next button.

Access will now display the first record found with Jones in the *LastName* field. If the Mr. Jones in the displayed client record were not the Jones you were seeking, you could click the Find Next button until you located the correct record.

5.   Close the Find dialog and then close the No Fault Travel Database.

Skill Builder: Lesson #6

1.   Open the *Employees* database.

2.   Use the Form Design to create a form named *Employee Entry/Edit form* that is based on all fields in the *Employees* table.

3.   Build the form so that is appears as the form below:

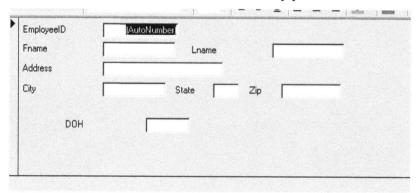

4.   Enter the following records using the new form:

Sam Martinez	Rosa Jackson	Marty Scarioni
454 Daisy	233 First St.	9043 Apple
Boise, ID 83705	Ontario, OR 93333	Nampa, ID 83555
2/13/97	7/12/99	10/22/00

5.   Use the Form Wizard to create a tabular form based on the *Positions* table. Make any needed design changes and then save this form as *Employee Positions.*

6.   Add the following records to that table:

Title	Department	Supervisor	DIP	PayRate	EmployeeID
Secretary	Admin	Jones	1/2/99	$14.22	1
Admin Assistant	Admin	Anderson	8/12/99	$15.55	1
Programmer	IT	Sandoval	12/22/99	$19.00	2

7.   Close the database when done.

Lesson #7: Creating and Using Select Queries

In this lesson you will learn to:

Create Select Queries
Add Criteria to Select Queries
Use the Date() Function

Lesson #7: Creating and Using Select Queries

Select queries allow you to filter or select which records you want to view. You can add conditions or criteria to queries to see specific records. Select queries can be saved and used as the basis for reports or even mailing labels.

In this lesson you will create select queries and learn how to add criteria to select specific records.

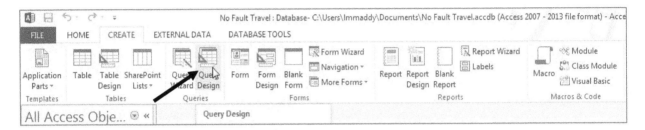

1.   Open the *No Fault Travel* database. Click the Create tab. Select Query Design in the Queries group.

The Show Table dialog box should appear where you can choose the Table(s) you wish to use in this query.

3.   Choose the *Clients* table and then click Add.

You will create this first query based only on the Clients table.

4.   Close the Show Table dialog box.

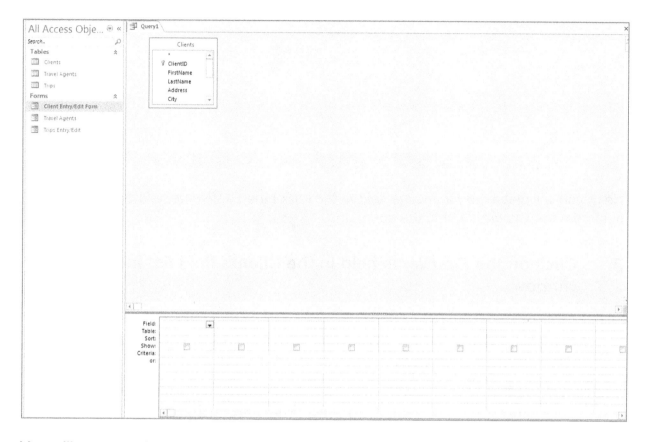

You will now see the query grid. The top section of the query window displays a list of fields for each table you selected to use for this query.

Adding Fields to the Query Grid

The next step in creating a query is to choose the fields you want to use in the query. You choose the fields which you will use later to identify which records you want to display.

You can add fields to the grid in three ways: 1) double-clicking on the field in the table field list, 2) dragging the field from the table field list down to the query grid, or 3) selecting the field from the Field drop down list in the grid. In the following exercise, you will use these methods to select which fields to use in the query.

1.   Double-click the *LastName* field in the Clients field list.

The *LastName* field should appear in the first column of the query grid.

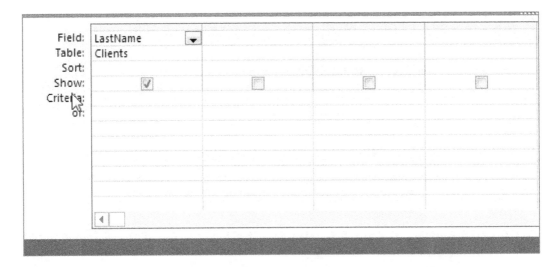

Next, you will place the *FirstName* field to the left of the *LastName* field by dragging the field from the *Clients* list onto the query grid.

2.   **Click on the *FirstName* field in the Clients field list in the query window.**

3.   **Carefully drag the *FirstName* field directly onto the *LastName* field in the query grid.**

You should see that Access inserted the *FirstName* field in front of the *LastName* field. Double-clicking to add fields to the query grid places them in the next available column. Dragging the fields from the field list allows you to place them in a specific column.

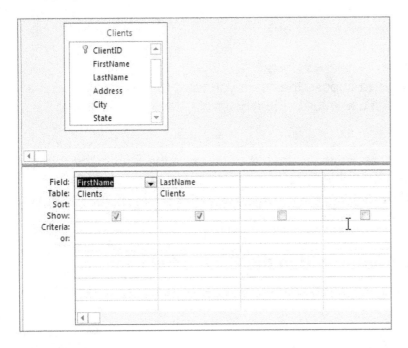

5. **Add the *Address, City, State*, and *Zip* fields to the query grid by dragging or double-clicking them.**

You can also add a field to a query by clicking the drop down arrow in the Field (top) row in the grid. You will add the *ActiveCustomer* field to the query using this method.

6. **If needed, use the horizontal scroll bar in the query window to scroll to the grid column after *Zip*.**

7. **Click in the top row labeled Field in the blank column after the *Zip* column.**

8. **Click the down arrow, so that the drop-down list containing the field names for the *Clients* table appears. Scroll down to and choose *ActiveCustomer*.**

You can use the drop down list to add any field from the selected table(s) to your query.

Viewing Query Results

To view the results of a query you can click the View tool on the ribbon. Access displays the query results in Datasheet View. At this point, you have selected the fields you want to use, but you have not specified any conditions for those fields which will allow you to view only records meeting that criteria.

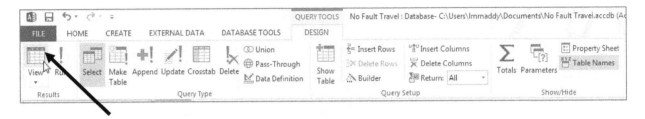

1. From the active Query Tools Design tab, click the View tool in the Results group.

Access displays the query in Datasheet View. You will see a "null" record in the query which is not a record; it displays the default values you have set for the *State* and *ActiveCustomer* fields. If you look at the record navigation bar at the bottom of the window, it indicates there are only four records in this query result table.

FirstName	LastName	Address	City	State	Zip	ActiveCusto
Robert	Johnson	88 Almond	Boise	ID	83706-1211	☑
Becky	Adams	203 Pinewood	Boise	ID	83441-	☑
Alvin	Black	88 Fern	Caldwell	ID	83655-	☑
Robert	Jones	22 Oakridge	Nyssa	OR	85112-	☐
*				ID		☑

Record: I◄ ◄ 1 of 4 ► ►I ►⊞ 🏺 No Filter   Search

Sorting the Query Result

As you view the query result, you will notice the records are sorted by the *ClientID* field (not included in the table because you did not select this field). By default, Access sorts the records in both a table and query result by the primary key. You can easily change the order within the query.

1.   **Click the View tool on the Home tab to return to the Design View of the query.**

2.   **In the *LastName* field, click the drop-down arrow in the Sort row.**

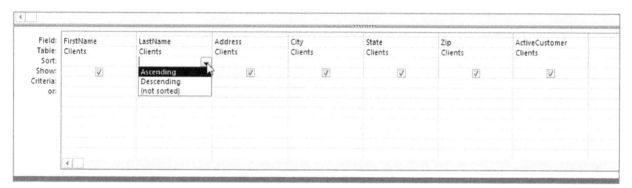

3.   **Choose Ascending from the drop-down list of sort choices.**

You should notice the Sort row in the *LastName* column now displays Ascending, meaning the query will be sorted based on ascending order (A to Z) of this field.

4.   **Click the View tool again to view the query result.**

This time the records in the query are sorted by last name.

Selecting Records in a Query

The query result is displaying all records in the *Client* table. Queries are so powerful because they allow you to specify only select records based on field criteria you add. In the next steps, you will specify that you only want to view records for active customers.

There are several methods of specifying criteria in fields. The criteria you enter also depends on the field's data type; as an example, only Yes or No would be valid criteria in a YES/NO field.

You can specify exact or relational values as criteria for number and currency fields. As an example, entering *>200* as criteria for a *Cost* field would cause Access to display only the records with a value greater than 200 in the *Cost* field. Math symbols which can be used as criteria in number and currency fields include:

<	less than
>	greater than
<=	less than or equal to
>=	greater than or equal to
*	Wild Card character used to specify part of a field

There are other techniques and operators that you can use when building criteria and you will use some of these as you continue with this lesson.

1.   Return to the Design View of the query.

You can do this by clicking the View tool on the Home tab.

2.   Move to the criteria row of the *ActiveCustomer* column.

You may need to use the horizontal scroll bar to scroll to this column.

3.   Type *YES* in the criteria row.

You will usually see YES/NO fields, such as *ActiveCustomer* displayed with the checkbox option. A check in the checkbox indicates yes and the absence of a checkbox indicates no. In the criteria, you enter the exact value you want to use to filter the records.

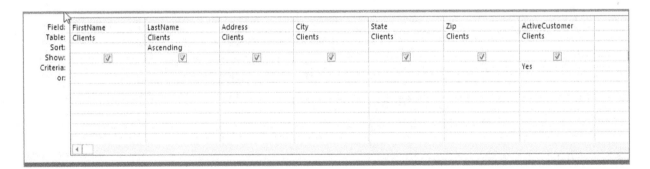

4.   Click the View tool on the Home tab.

You are now viewing the results of the query with criteria you set. You should notice that one record, Robert Jones is not displayed in this query because he is not an active cutomer. The record count on the navigation bar should show only three records.

Saving a Query

After creating a query, you will usually want to save it. Saving the query lets you use the same criteria to view records at a later time. Saving the query also lets you create reports based on the query.

Each time you open a saved query, you are viewing current data. In other words, if more active clients were added to the *Clients* table, they would also appear in the query result. Each time you open the query, it reflects the current data in the database. Saving a query does not cause it to display only the records at the time the query was created and saved. The query will change as the records in the database change.

1.   Click on the Save tool on the Quick Access toolbar.

2.   In the Save As dialog box, type *Clients Currently Active* in the Query Name text box and click OK.

3.   Close the query but leave the database open.

Using Additional Criteria in Queries

The real power in queries lies in their ability to select only certain records depending on the criteria that you enter. In this portion of the lesson you will explore different methods of entering criteria.

1.   Select the Create tab, then click Query Design on the ribbon.

2.   Add the *Clients* table and then close the Show Table dialog box.

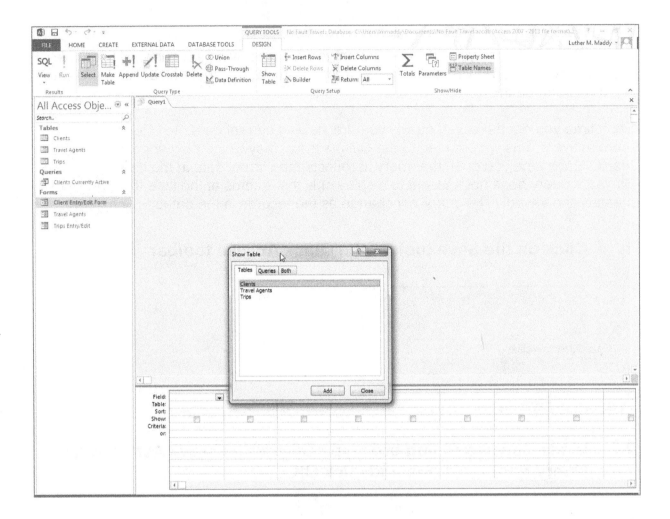

3.   **Add the following fields to the query grid using any of the three methods you previously learned.**

> FirstName
> LastName
> City
> DOB

You will now add criteria to select records in which the *City* field contains first a specific city and then later either of two specified cities.

4.   **Move to the criteria row in the City field.**

5.   **Type *Boise* in this row and press (Enter)**

Notice that Access added quotation marks ("") around Boise because criteria for text fields requires quotation marks. Access added them for you because the *City* field is a text field.

6. Click the View tool to view the query in Data sheet View.

The only records you should see in this list are those with Boise in the city field.

7. Switch back to Design View.

You can return directly to Design View by clicking on the Design View tool in the Views group on the Home tab on the ribbon. When you are in Datasheet View, the Design View tool is on the ribbon; when you are in Design View, the Datasheet View is on the ribbon.

8. Move back to the criteria row of the City field and erase the current criteria.

You can easily erase existing criteria by moving into the cell and pressing (Esc). This will select all cell contents. You can then press (Delete) to erase the existing criteria.

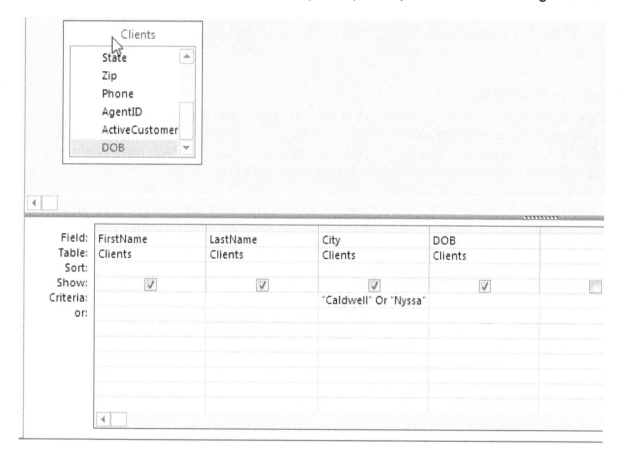

9. In the Criteria row of the City field type *Caldwell or Nyssa* and press (Enter).

Access will automatically add quotation marks around both cities. Access recognizes the Or in the criteria as an operator and does not add quotation marks.

10.   Switch to Datasheet View.

You should now see only those records that live in <u>either</u> Caldwell or Nyssa.

11.   Return to the Design View and then erase the criteria in the City field.

12.   After erasing the criteria, type *not Boise* in the Criteria row of the City Field and then run the query.

The NOT operator allows you to select all records except those listed in the NOT statement for the field criteria. In this case, all records except those with Boise in the *City* field.

13.   When done, close the query without saving.

Using the Date() Function

For example, if you wish to create a list of trips scheduled to depart in the next 30 days, will you base the criteria on a date range. An easy way to create a date range is to use the BETWEEN operator. The BETWEEN operator is inclusive, which means the two dates defining the between range will also be included in the range.

If you want to use a query at a later time, avoid placing the actual dates in the criteria. "Hard coding" dates makes a query obsolete when the date changes and would require you to change the criteria every time you use it.

You can use the Date() function instead. This function returns the current date.

1.   Click the Create tab, and then the Query Design tool to create a new query.

2.   Select the *Trips* table in the Show Table dialog box, and then close the dialog box.

3.   Add the fields: *ClientID, Destination, Cost, DepartureDate and ReturnDate.*

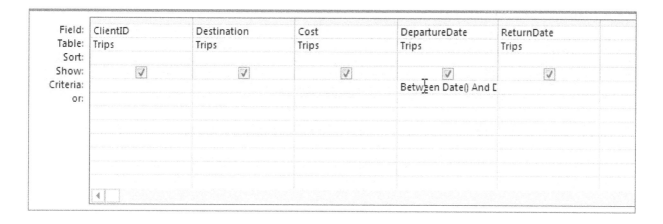

4. **Move to the Criteria row of the *DepartureDate* field and type *between date() and date()+30* and press (Enter).**

With this criteria, only records with trips departing in the next 30 days are selected. If you entered all departure dates as earlier than today when you entered the data in the *Trips* table, this query will return no records.

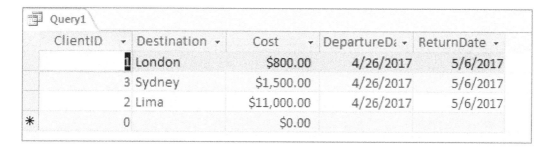

5. **Click the DataSheet View tool to display the results of this query.**

You should see only the trips specified in your criteria. If you do not see the records you expected, open the *Trips* table and edit some departure dates as today's date.

The dates in your records will be different from those shown above.

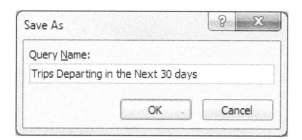

6. **Save this query as *Trips departing in the next 30 days* and then Close the query.**

Creating Queries Based on Related Tables

In order to see fields from two different tables, such as a client's name and the details of the client's trip, you must create a query based on more than one table. However, when you create queries based on related tables the only records that appear in the query result are the records that are related to each other.

For example, if you create a query in the *No Fault Travel* database based on the *Clients* and *Trips* tables, the only clients in the query result will be clients with information in the *Trips* table. Similarly, if you create a query based on *Travel Agents* and *Clients*, the only clients in a query result are those with an assigned travel agent. Likewise, the only travel agents included are those with clients assigned to them.

In the last part of this lesson, you will create a query based on related tables. Even though you will not add any criteria, Access will automatically exclude records that are not related.

1.   Click the Create tab, and then select Query Design tool on the ribbon.

2.   Choose the *Clients* table and then close the Show Table dialog box.

3.   Add the *FirstName* and *LastName* fields to the query.

Remember, to add fields you can double-click, drag, or use the drop-down list in the Field row of the query grid.

4.   Click the View tool to see the result of this query and verify that all clients display in the query result.

Now, you will add the *Trips* table to this query. By doing so you will eliminate all the clients who have no records in the *Trips* table.

5.   Click the View tool to return to Design View.

6.   **On the Query Tools Design tab, click the Show Table tool in the Query Setup group.**

It is easy to open the Show Table dialog box again and to add additional tables to a query.

7.   **Select the *Trips* table and then click Add.**

8.   **After adding the *Trips* table, click Close to close the Show Table dialog box.**

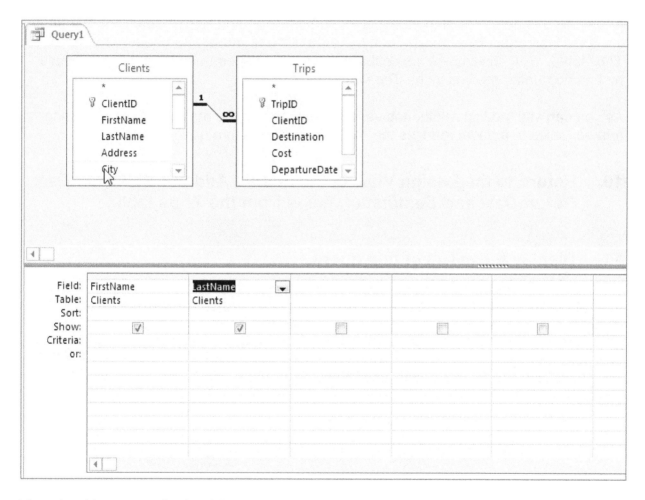

You should now see both tables in the query grid. The join line informs you that the two tables are related by a relationship you created in a previous lesson.

9.   **Without adding any additional fields, click the View tool to see the result of the query.**

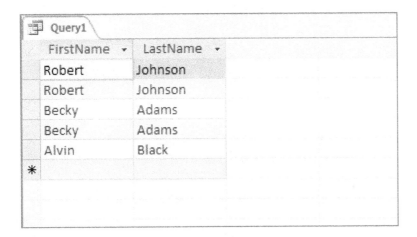

In viewing this query result, notice that Robert Johnson and Becky Adams appear in the list more than once. Mr. Johnson and Ms. Adams have more than one record in the *Trips* table. You should also notice that Robert Jones does not appear at all because he has no related records in the *Trips* table.

As you can see, adding related tables to a query affects the result. Normally, adding related tables to a query reduces the number of records in a query result.

10. Return to the Design View of the query. Add the *DepartureDate*, *ReturnDate* and *Destination* fields from the *Trips* table.

11. Display the result of this query.

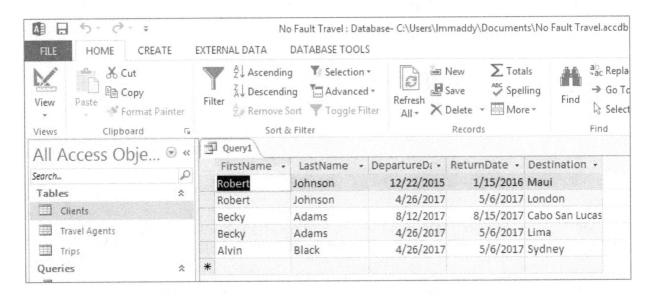

Additional information for each trip is now displayed.

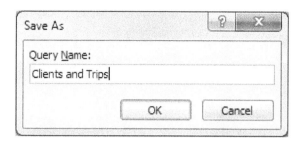

12. **Save this query as *Clients and Trips* and then close the query.**

13. **Close the No Fault Travel database.**

Skill Builder: Lesson #7

1.   Open the Employees database

2.   Create a query that displays only the employees living in Idaho.

3.   Save this query as *Employees living in Idaho.*

4.   Create a query that shows only those employees hired after 12/31/1997.

5.   Save this query as *Employees hired after 1997.*

6.   Create a query that lists each employee's name and all fields from the Positions table.

7.   Save this query as *Employees and Positions* and view the result.

8.   Why doesn't every employee appear in this query?

9.   Close the *Employees* database.

Lesson #8: Creating and Using Reports

In this lesson you will learn to:

Use the Report Wizard
Use the Mailing Label Wizard
Base Reports on Queries

Lesson #8: Creating and Using Reports

Reports are usually lists of information presented in column form. With Reports, you can display the information in tables or queries with additional formatting and features such as totals and sub-totals. Reports are very flexible and can be used to create and print mailing labels.

In this lesson, you will create reports which total numeric values. You will also create mailing labels.

Steps in Creating Reports

The first steps are: 1) determining which fields you want to include, 2) how you want the report formatted, and 3) deciding which records you want to appear on the report.

After determining the fields and records you wish to display on the report, the next step is often to create a query that provides you with those fields and records.

The final step is often to use a report wizard to build the report you envision, based on the query you created just for that report.

Using the Label Wizard

The Label Wizard will quickly help you through the process of creating a mailing label or some other label type. In the following exercise, you will create mailing labels for all clients flagged as "Active" in the *Clients* table of the *No Fault Travel* database. You will use the query you created earlier which displays the names and addresses of the active clients.

1.   **Open the No Fault Travel database.**

2.   **Click the query named, *Clients Currently Active,* in the All Access Objects pane to select it.**

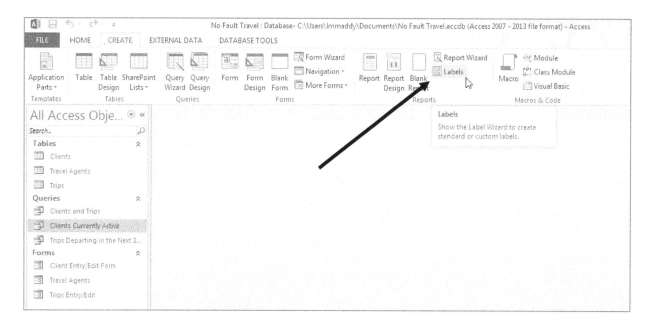

The Label Wizard will help you create labels for the selected table or query.

3.   Display the Create tab.

4.   Click the Labels tool in the Reports group.

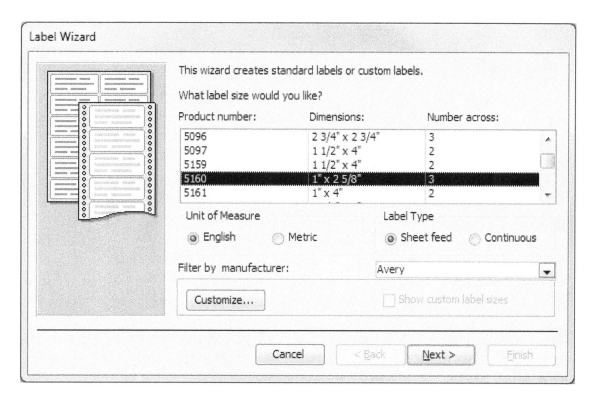

In the Label Wizard dialog box, you will first choose the label type that you are using.

1. **In the text box next to Filter by manufacturer, click the drop-down list button and select Avery.**

2. **Make sure that the English radio button is selected under Unit of Measure.**

3. **Under Product number (for Avery labels), choose 5160 and click Next.**

The label size you have selected is a standard mailing label. When you create your own labels, you can select a different size. If the manufacturer of your label is not listed, you can use the label's measurements to select a label with the same label size, or you can customize your own label.

Access will now ask you to choose the font and text color on the labels.

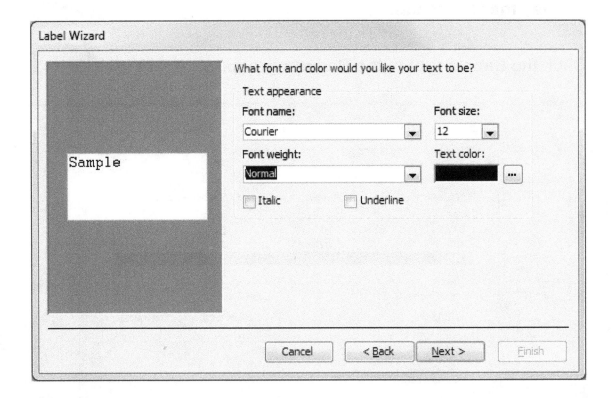

4. **Choose Courier as the Font name, 12 point as the Font size, and Normal as the Font weight. Leave the text color as Black and then click Next.**

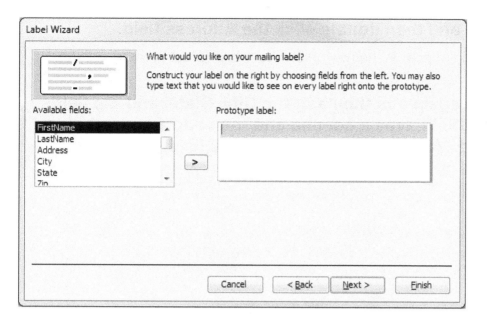

You will now lay out the fields as you want them to appear on the mailing label.

5.   Double-click the *FirstName* field.

You should see this field added to the Prototype label.

6.   Press (space) and then double click the LastName field.

You pressed the space bar so that a space appears between the two fields on the printed labels.

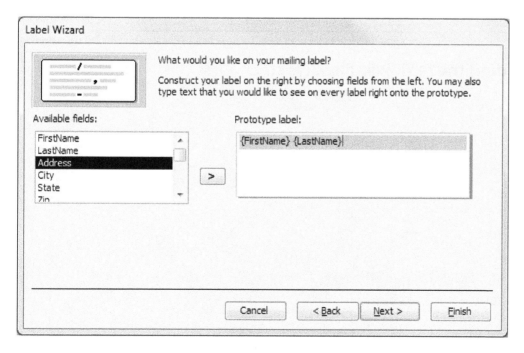

7. **Press (Enter) and then double click the Address field.**

The *Address* field should appear in the row below the first and last names.

8. **Press (Enter) again and then add the City, State, and Zip fields. After the City field, type a comma and then add a space before the State field. Add a space after the State field.**

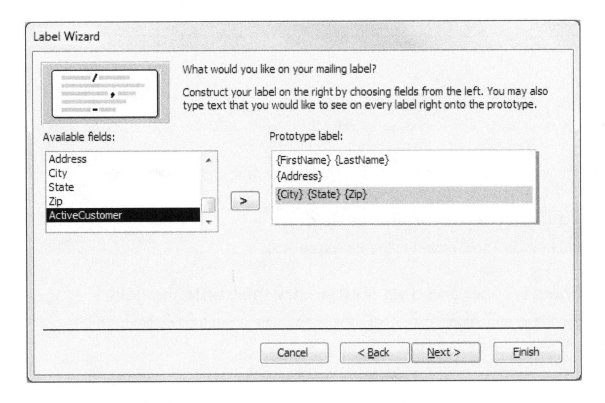

9. **After adding these fields, click Next.**

In this dialog box, you will specify how you want the labels sorted.

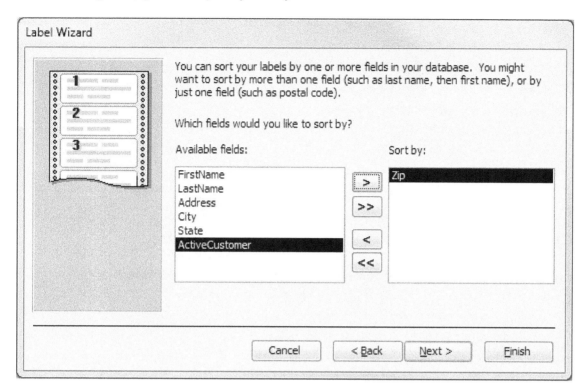

10. **Double-click the *Zip* field to add it to the Sort by field list, and then click Next.**

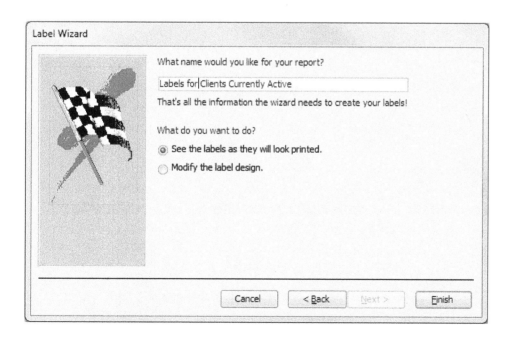

11. **Name this report, *Labels for Clients Currently Active* and then click Finish.**

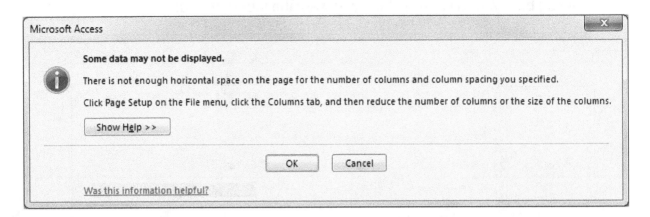

If you see the above Microsoft Access message, click OK. Access is simply warning you that your printer and label size might not be perfectly compatible.

You should now see mailing labels for the three active clients in this database.

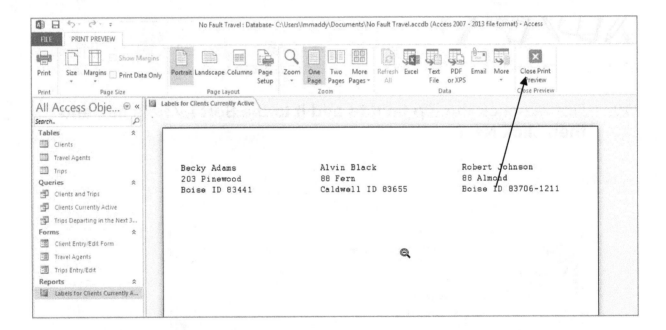

12.   Click the Close Print Preview button on the Print Preview tab ribbon.

13.   Close the Label report.

Using the Report Wizard

You will now use the Report Wizard to create a report that lists every trip that each client has taken or booked. This report will also total the cost of all the trips for each client.

You do not need to create a query to build this report because the limiting criteria you want will be automatically built-in to the report, as you add fields of the related tables to the report. Since you will base the report on two tables, *Clients* and *Trips*, only the clients who have taken or scheduled trips will appear in this report.

1. **Click on the *Clients* table in the All Access Objects pane to select it. Click the Create tab, and then select the Report Wizard tool in the Reports group.**

Unlike the Label Wizard, the Report Wizard allows you to easily select one or more tables to be used in the report. Selecting the *Clients* table before opening the Report Wizard simply saved a step in the report creation process.

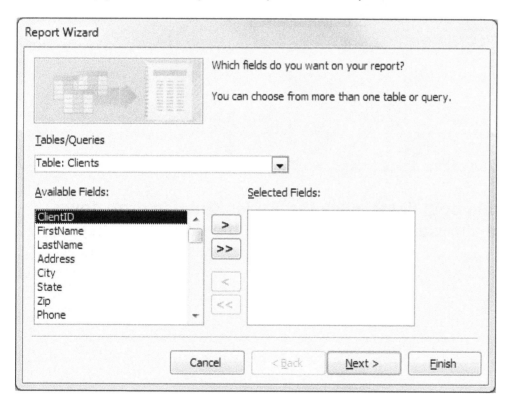

2. **Make sure that the *Clients* table is displayed in the Tables/Queries drop-down list.**

If you selected the *Clients* table before clicking the Report Wizard, the *Clients* table is selected when you open the wizard. If not, you can use the drop-down list for Tables/Queries to choose the *Clients* table. After choosing the table, you will choose the fields you want included on the report and the order that the fields should appear.

3.   Double-click on the *LastName* field and then the *FirstName* field.

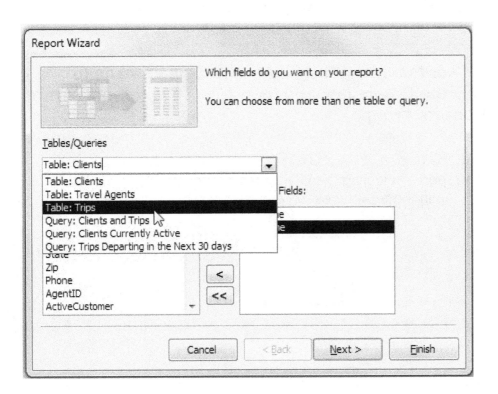

4.   After adding both fields, click the Tables/Queries drop down arrow and choose the *Trips* table from the drop-down list.

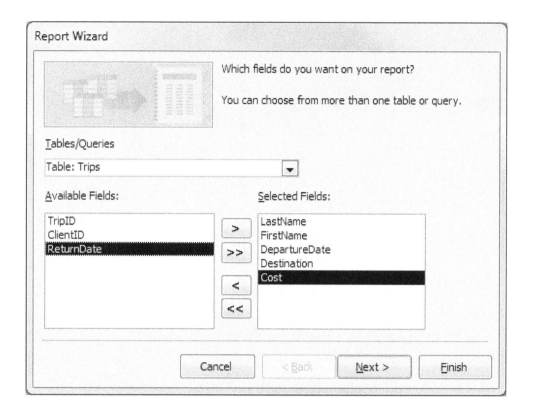

5.   **From the *Trips* field list, add *DepartureDate*, *Destination* and *Cost* by double-clicking each field.**

The Report Wizard allows you to choose fields from different tables. In doing so, you will only see the clients who have trips because you are using two related tables. If you wanted to filter the records further, for example, to list only the clients who scheduled trips to Maui, you should first create a query and then the report.

6.   **After adding these fields, click Next.**

Access now asks how you want to view the data in this report. Leaving this as view by Clients will allow you to subtotal the cost of the trips for each client.

7.   **Click Next when Access asks how you want to view the data in this report.**

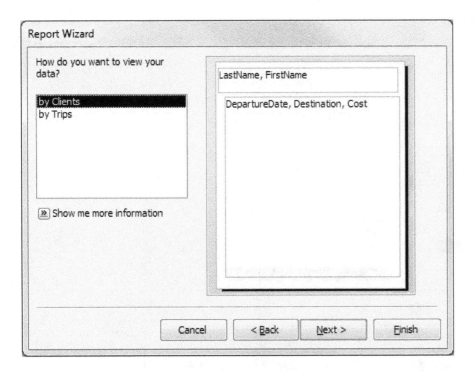

Access now asks if you want to add any grouping levels. You want this report to be grouped by clients as it already is, so you will not make any changes here.

6.   Click Next, when Access asks if you want to add any additional grouping levels.

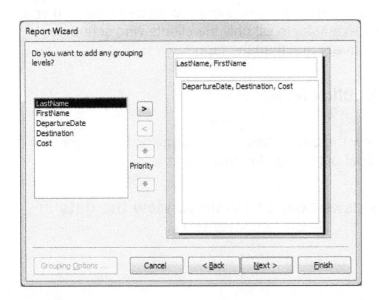

Access now asks how you how you want the information sorted. The report will already be sorted by the client's name, but trips scheduled or taken by each client will be sorted by the departure date that you included from the *Trips* table.

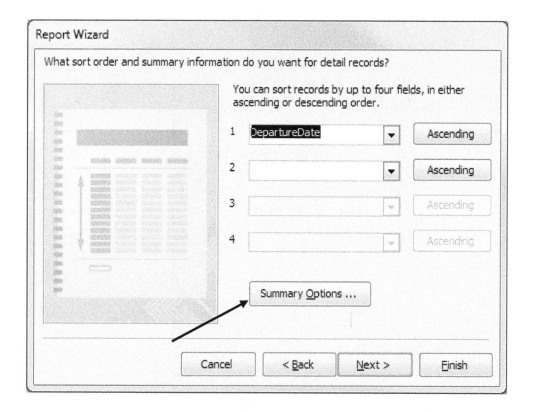

9. Choose *DepartureDate* in the first Sort text box.

For clients with multiple trips, the trips will be sorted by departure date.

This dialog box also asks you what summary information that you want included. You want this report to total the cost of each client's trips and to provide the grand total of all trips. You will do this by clicking the Summary Options button to open the Summary Options dialog box.

10. Click the Summary Options button in the Report Wizard dialog box.

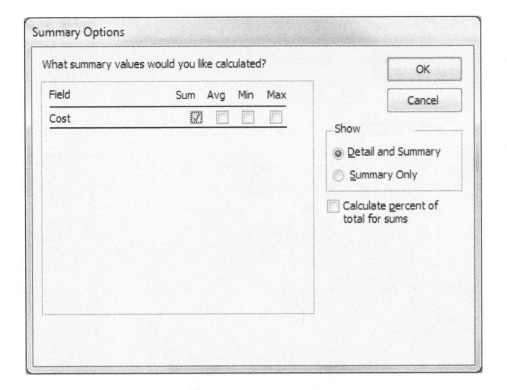

11.   Turn on the Sum checkbox and click OK.

Access will list all the numeric fields included in your report here. You can choose several calculations in the Summary Options dialog box.

12.   When you return to the sort specifications, click Next.

You will now specify the report layout. You can also select either portrait or landscape orientation.

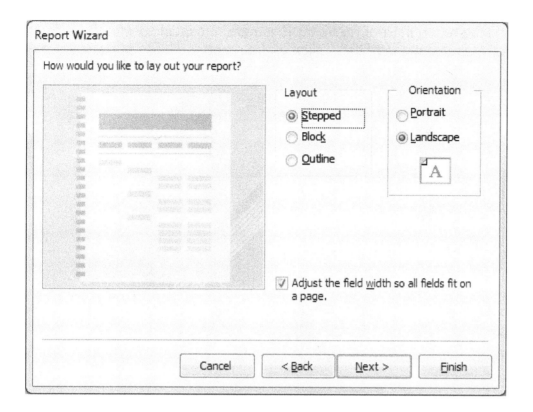

13. **Choose Stepped as the Layout and Landscape as the Orientation. Click Next.**

14. **Enter the name, *Clients and Trip Totals*, and click Finish.**

You are now viewing the report in Print Preview. If you are not satisfied with the report's appearance, you will make changes to the design of the report.

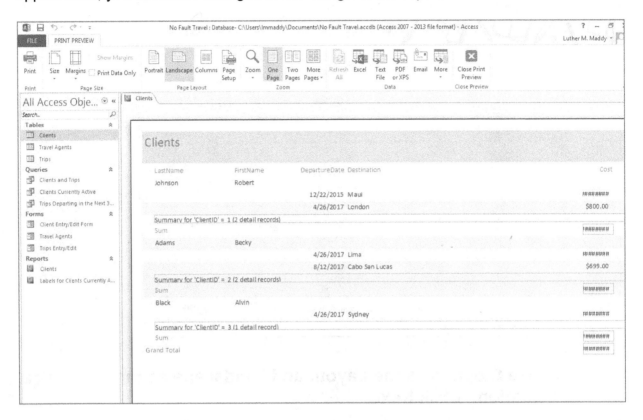

It is likely that you see #### instead of values in some cost and total fields. These characters (i.e., ####) appear because the report field widths are not large enough to display the information correctly. You will make these fields wider, as well as modify other aspects of this report.

Modifying the Report Design

To change a report's appearance, you will enter Design View and make changes, much like you did when you created the database forms. In Design View, you can change the position or size of fields and make other changes.

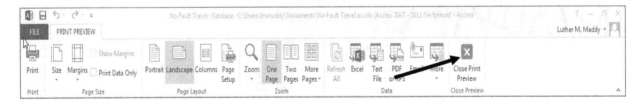

1.   After previewing the report, close Print Preview.

You are now viewing the report design. Notice this report has several sections: a report header and footer; a page header and footer; and the client header, footer and detail.

The Report Header and Footer appear once at the beginning and end of the report, respectively. The Page Header and Page Footer appear at the top and bottom of each page, respectively. The ClientID header and footer appear once for each client. The detail section displays the information for each client. The sections in our *Clients and Trips* report display the following:

Report Header	Report Title
Page Header	Field names (labels) for data in report
ClientID Header	Client's name
Detail	Trips scheduled for each client
ClientID Footer	Subtotal of trips scheduled by each client
Page Footer	Today's date and page number
Report Footer	Grand total of all trips scheduled

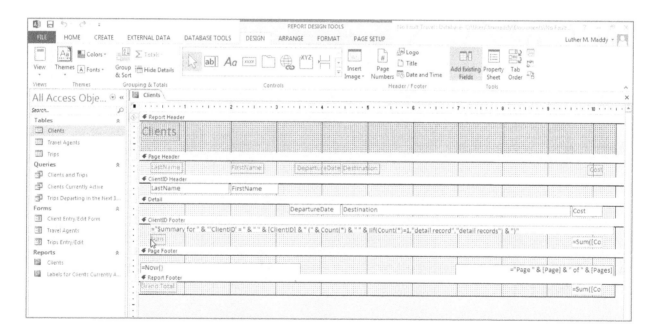

Notice the text boxes in ClientID header and detail. The report displays the selected data from the tables in the text boxes. The client's first and last names stored in the *Client* table are displayed in ClientID Header. The trip's departure date, destination, and cost stored in the *Trips* table are displayed in the Detail section.

2. **Select the *Destination* text box in the Detail section. Use the sizing handle at the right edge to decrease its width by 1 inch.**

Reminder: When the double-headed arrow appears, you can adjust the size.

You are making this field smaller so that you can increase the width of the *Cost* field and the *Cost* subtotal field.

3. **Select the following fields: Cost, =Sum[Cost] in ClientID Footer, and =Sum([Cost]) in Report Footer. Use the sizing handles on the left edge to increase the width by approximately 3/4 inch.**

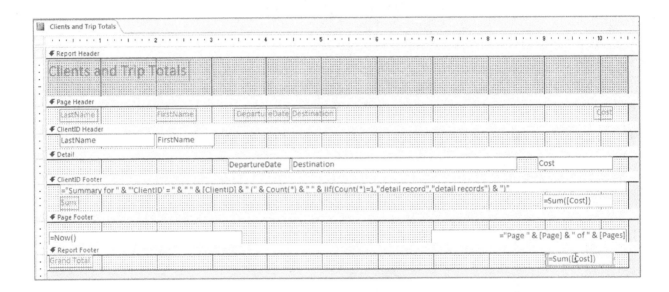

4. **Save the modified report and then select Print Preview from the View tool.**

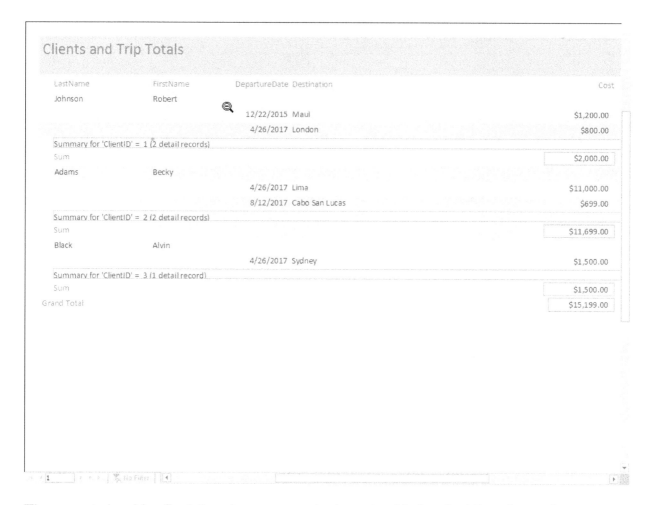

The report should reflect the changes you just made. Notice that the clients do not appear in alphabetical order. This is because the report is sorted by client ID. If you want the report sorted by client's last name, you would need to create a query to control sorting, and use the query results to generate the report.

5. Close the report and the No Fault Travel database.

Skill Builder: Lesson #8

1. Open the *Employee* database.

2. Create a report that prints mailing labels for all the Employees.

3. Save this report as *Employee Mailing Labels*.

4. Use a query and the Report Wizard to create a report that lists each employee and the positions each has held but only within the *Admin* department.

5. Save this report as *Admin Employees and Positions*.

Lesson #9: Combo Boxes and Form Enhancements

In this lesson you will learn to:

Add Enhancements to Forms
Add Combo Boxes to a Form

Lesson #9: Combo Boxes and Form Enhancements

In this lesson you will add elements to forms. You will also create combo boxes that allow you to lookup information from other tables when entering or editing data.

1. **Open the *No Fault Travel* database.**

2. **Display the *Client Entry/Edit* Form in Design View**

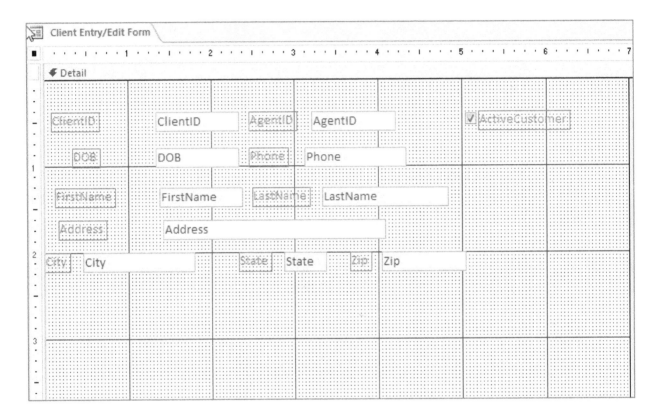

Using the Controls Group

To add combo boxes and other form elements, you will need to use the Controls group. You will find the Controls group on the Form Design Tools Design tab on the ribbon.

3. **If the Controls group is not already displayed, click the Design tab under Form Design Tools.**

4. **Use the vertical ruler to select all the controls in the detail section of the form.**

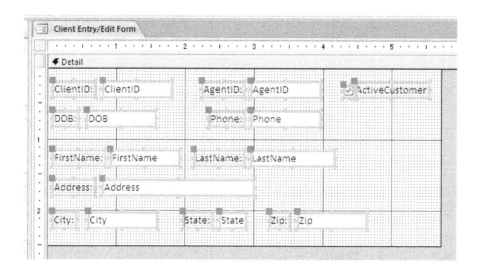

When you move the mouse pointer to the vertical ruler, the pointer will become a black arrow. If you drag the black arrow on the vertical ruler from the form's top to bottom, all controls will be selected.

5. **Point to any control, until the mouse pointer becomes a four-headed arrow. (Avoid close proximity to the sizing handles.)**

The four-headed arrow will move all selected controls.

6. **Drag the controls down so that the top of the first row is approximately at the 1" vertical position.**

It may be necessary to increase the height of your form.

You will now use the Controls group to insert a label control at the top of this form. This label will serve as a title for viewing and printing.

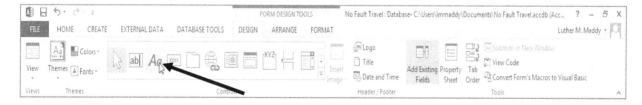

1. **Locate and click the Label control.**

You do not need to drag this control. Just click on it to select it. Then move the mouse to the desired location on the form and click. Once the mouse pointer is moved to the form, the pointer changes to represent the label tool.

2. Move the mouse pointer to the top left corner of the detail section and click.

If you move the mouse pointer off the form, the mouse pointer transforms to a no-entry symbol. Move back on the form, and click when you see the large letter "A". When you click, a tiny label appears with a blinking insertion point (cursor) where you can type the text you want displayed.

3. Type *Client Information Form* in the label and press (Enter).

You may notice that warning symbol appears and opens a message that the label is an unbound control (i.e., not associated with any data).

You should the see sizing handles on label control, which indicate that the label is selected and you can make changes to its appearance.

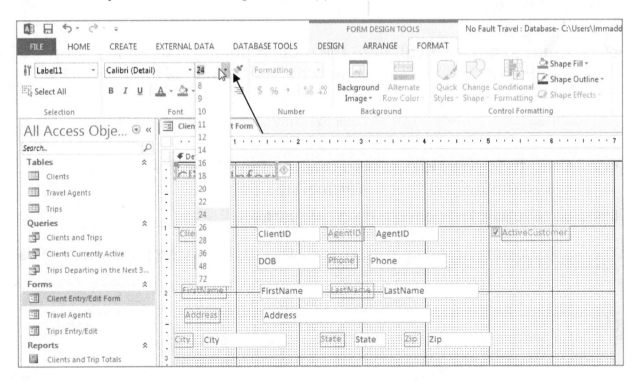

4. With the new label still selected, display the Form Design Tools Format tab. Change font size to 24 points.

The text font size increases, but the label control itself does not increase in size, so the text is no longer visible. In the next steps, you will have Access automatically adjust the size of the label control to fit the larger text.

5.   Display the Format Design Tools Arrange tab.

6.   Click the Size/Space tool and choose To Fit on the drop-down menu.

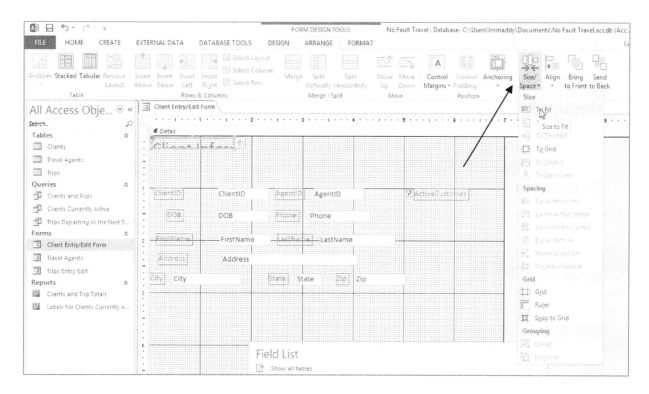

The complete text should now be visible in the resized label control.

7.   With the control still selected, drag the label to the top center of the form.

The horizontal and vertical rulers are helpful in positioning controls, but you do not need to be exact in this exercise.

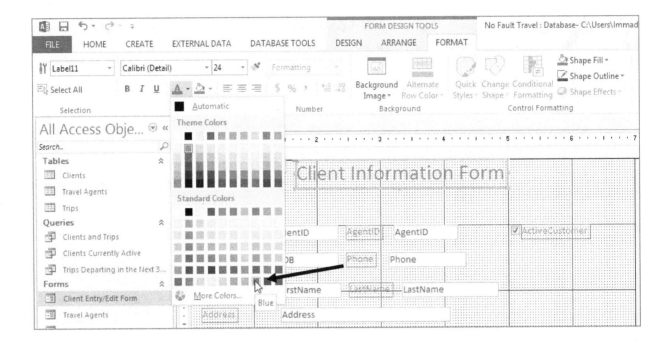

8. Click the Form Design Tools Format tab. Next click the drop-down arrow for font color. Select Blue in the drop-down color options.

The label text should now be blue.

Creating a Combo Box

A combo box is a drop-down list that can appear on a form. Using a combo box, the data to be entered is selected from a list, instead of typed. Combo boxes are very useful for data entry and editing. In this part of the lesson, you will create a combo box that looks up and displays all travel agents in the *Travel Agents* table.

1. Click on the *AgentID* text box and press (Delete).

The text box is the "white box". Deleting the text box will also delete the associated control *AgentID* label. You deleted this field because you will replace it with a combo box that looks up the travel agents directly from the *Travel Agents* table.

2. Display the Format Design Tools Design tab. Then, locate and click the Combo Box tool on the Controls group.

As you move the mouse pointer over the form, the pointer transforms its shape to represent the combo box tool. The plus (+) shows you where the box's top left corner will be located when you click. A label control will also appear to the left of the combo box, so you also need to make sure that there will be enough space for the label.

3. Move the mouse pointer just to the right of where the *AgentID* text box was located, and click.

The plus (+) should be about 3.75" from the left page side. Do not worry about being exact. You will adjust the combo box's position later in this exercise. When you click, the Combo Box Wizard opens.

The Combo Box Wizard asks you if the values to be displayed are in another table (or query) or if you want to type in the values. In this case, the *Travel Agent* table has the values you want to display.

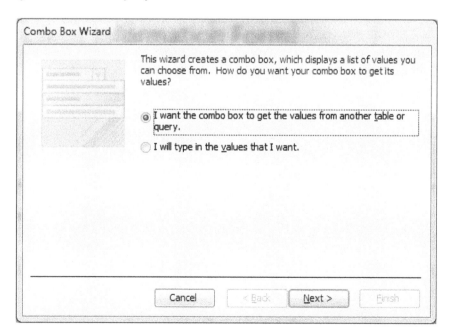

4.   In the Combo Box Wizard, make sure that the option of getting the values from another table is selected. Click Next.

The next screen asks you to select the table containing the values you want to look up.

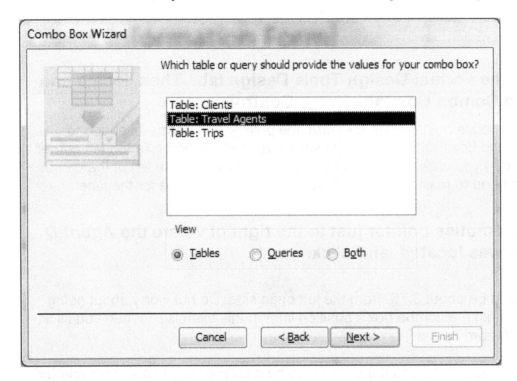

5.   Choose the *Travel Agents* table and click Next.

Access now asks which fields you want to display in the combo box. In this example, the *AgentID* field is the value you want. However, having the combo box display the travel agent's name will help ensure you select the correct agent ID value.

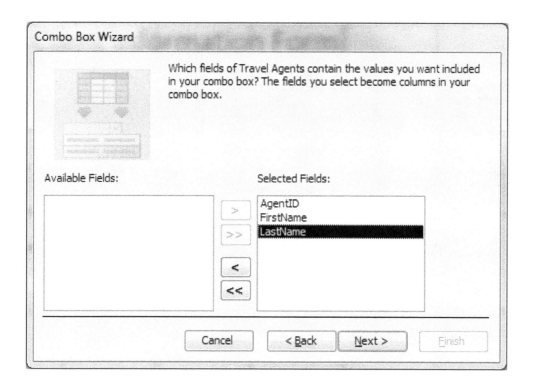

6. **Click the double arrows (>>) to add all the fields in this table. Click Next.**

You will have Access use all three fields in this combo box.

7. **Click Next when asked how you want to sort the list.**

Access will now display a sample combo box list. By default, the primary key is not displayed, so the agent ID field is not visible. If you wanted to lookup agents by name, this would be a good choice. However, in this case, you need to look up the Agent ID, so you will have Access display all three fields.

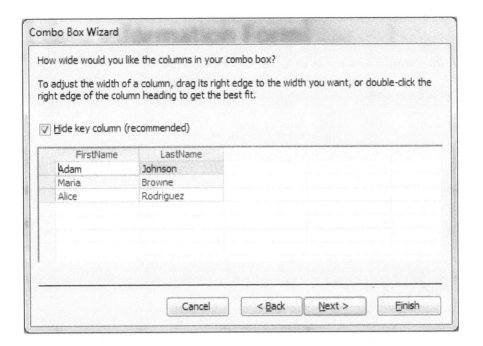

7.   Uncheck the checkbox for Hide key column.

Access will now display all three columns. You can manually adjust the column widths here by dragging the column edges. You can also double-click each column's right border, so that Access automatically adjusts it for "best fit".

8.   Adjust the column widths as desired and click Next.

The Combo Box Wizard now asks which of the three fields contains the value you want to store or use.

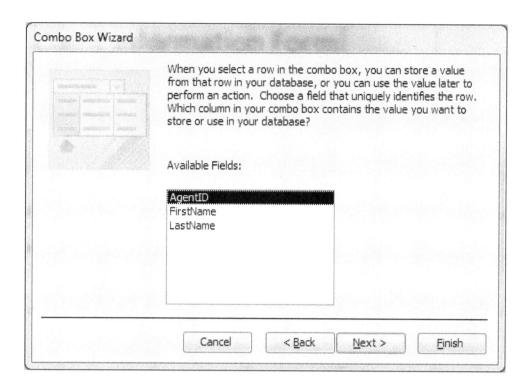

9.   Select the *AgentID* field and click Next.

The Combo Box Wizard now asks where you want to store the value. In this case, you have looked up the value from the *AgentID* field in *Travel Agents* table, and you are storing this value in a field in the *Clients* table with the same field name, *AgentID*.

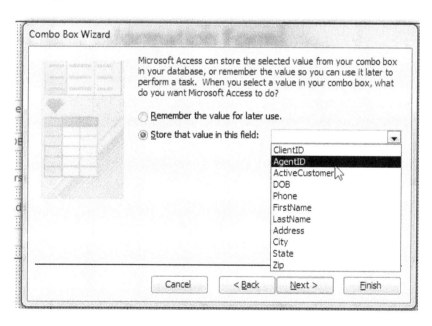

10.   Click the drop-down arrow and choose *AgentID* from the drop-down list. Click Next.

The final Combo Box Wizard screen asks you to label the combo box.

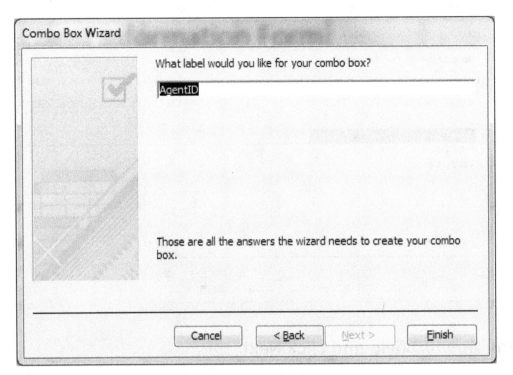

11. Make sure that *AgentID* is the label text and click Finish.

Aligning Controls

You should now see the combo box and label. You will now use the Align command in Access to align the labels and text boxes. To align controls you will select the controls you want to align and then choose how you want the controls aligned. In this portion of the lesson you will left align several label controls. When you choose the Left Align command, Access will align the controls to the one that is farthest to the left.

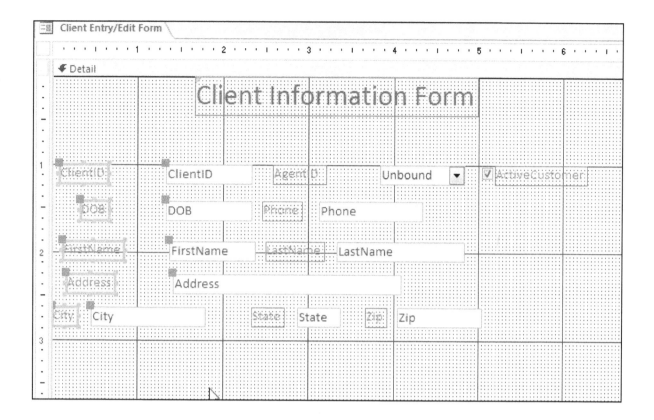

1. Select the label controls for *ClientID*, *DOB*, *FirstName*, *Address*, and *City*.

You can select multiple controls by selecting the first control and then holding down the (Shift) key as you select the remaining label controls.

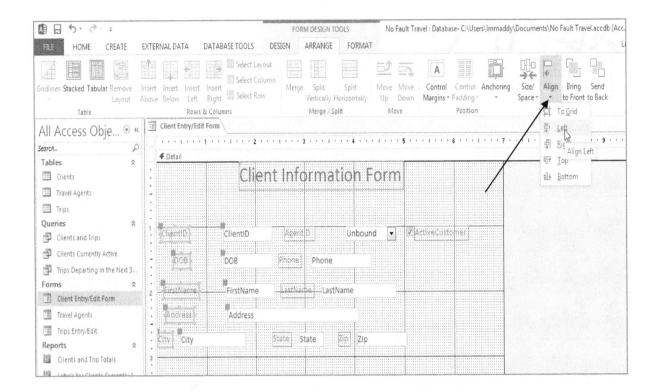

2.   **With the labels selected, display the Form Design Tools Arrange tab and click the Alignment tool. Choose Left from the alignment options.**

The labels should now all be perfectly aligned. You will now align the text boxes for these fields.

3.   **Select the City text box.**

4.   **Move the *City* text box so that its left edge is 1" from the left side of the form.**

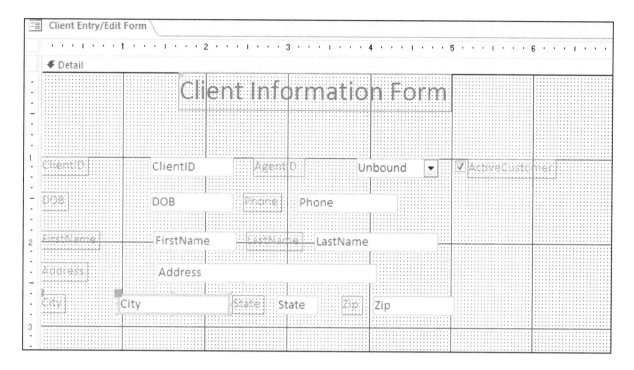

You can move a single control by dragging the upper left corner of the control.

5.   Now select the text boxes for *City*, *Address*, *FirstName*, *DOB*, and *ClientID*.

Use the (Shift) key to select multiple controls. You can also double-click the vertical (or horizontal) ruler to select all controls directly under (or to the right).

6.   On the Form Design Tools Arrange tab, click the Align tool and choose Align Left.

The text box controls should be perfectly aligned to the leftmost control, the *City* text box, in our case.

You are now ready to test your redesigned form.

7.   Save the form. Click the View tool on the Form Design Tools Design tab, to view the form.

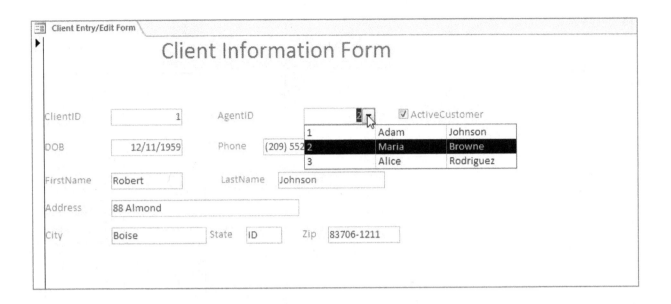

8. **Verify that the *AgentID* combo box works correctly, by changing the Agent for one or two clients.**

9. **Save the form and then close the database.**

Skill Builder: Lesson #9

1.   Open the *Employees* database.

2.   Go to the *Employee Entry* form in design view.

3.   If needed, use the Align command to align the labels and text boxes on the left side of this form.

4.   Change font colors and sizes to enhance the appearance of this form.

5.   Add a label at the top of the detail section that displays *Employee Information.* Choose a font size of 18 points and center the label.

6.   Save and close this form.

7.   In Design View of the *Employee Positions Form*, change the *Department* field text box to a combo box that displays the three valid departments; *Admin, IT,* or Sales.

Hint: Choose the option to type the values you want to appear in the combo box.

8.   Save and close this form.

9.   Close the *Employees* database.

Index

Other books that may interest you

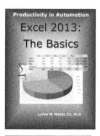

Excel: The Basics (2016, 2013 or 2010)
In "learning by doing" you will gain a good grasp of the basics of Excel. You'll learn to create formulas, format and print worksheets, copy and move cell data, and generate attractive charts and graphs from your Excel data.

Retail price: $10.95

Access: The Basics (2016, 2013)
In this course Access users will learn to: Understand Basic Database Design Techniques Create, Modify and Use Tables Create, Modify and Use Forms Create, Modify and Use Reports and Mailing Labels Create Database Relationships Enter, Edit, and Find Records Create, Edit and Use Queries Use Field Properties and Validation Rules Add Drop-down Lists to Forms

Retail price: $12.95

Excel: Database and Statistical Features (2016, 2013 or 2010)
In "learning by doing" you will gain a good grasp of the Excel database features. You'll learn to create and use Pivot Tables and Charts. You'll also learn about database functions like DSum() and DAverage(). You'll also learn about filtering and subtotaling Excel data. Finally, you'll learn about performing statistical analysis using the Analysis Toolpak.

Retail price: $9.95

Word: The Basics (2013 or 2010)
In "learning by doing" you will learn the basics of MS Word. You'll also be introduced to performing tasks the most efficient way possible to increase your productivity. This workbook covers document creation and editing. You'll learn to copy and move and enhance text. You'll also learn about page a paragraph formatting, setting tabs, creating tables and more.

2013: Retail price: $9.95   2010: Retail price: $8.95

Word: Enhancing Documents (2013 or 2010)
In "learning by doing" you will learn the some of the desktop publishing features of Word. You'll learn to place text in columns, use Autoshapes, enhance mailing labels, and use and create styles. You'll also learn to add hyperlinks to your documents, how to use pre-defined templates, and much more.

2013: Retail price: $9.95   2010: Retail price: $8.95

PowerPoint: The Basics (2016, 2013 or 2010)
In this "learning by doing" course you will learn to: Create and run presentations, Apply and modify design themes, Insert clipart, audio, and video clips, Apply and use slide transitions, Print audience handouts and speaker notes and much more

Retail price: $9.95

Order wherever books are sold. Ordering in quantity?
Save up to 20% by ordering on our website: **www.Pro-aut.com**